UWEM ESSIA

FISCAL DYNAMICS IN A TRANSFORMING GLOBAL ECONOMY

Contemporary Issues in Public Finance, the Future of Fiscal Policy, and Projections for 2060

To the policymakers shaping economic trajectories, the economists unraveling intricate theories, and the enthusiasts embracing the evolving dynamics of our global economy. Your dedication to understanding, adapting, and fostering positive change serves as an inspiration for future generations.

Contents

Preface

The book, "Fiscal Dynamics in a Transforming Global Economy" is a comprehensive exploration of the intricate world of public finance and its evolving dynamics in the digital era, with seven insightful chapters, each addressing critical facets of fiscal policies, monetary interactions, and the challenges and opportunities that shape our global economic landscape. The opening chapter, "Evolving Dynamics of Public Finance in the Digital Era," traverses the intricate threads of revenue collection, resource allocation, and asset/liability management. The chapter explores public finance's pivotal role in shaping economic policy and contributing to societal well-being.

Chapter Two: The Intersection of Public Finance and Monetary Policy discusses the monetary policy-fiscal policy intersection and how both sets of economic policies have to go together for economic stability and growth. Chapter Three, Evolution and Challenges of Fiscal Policy examines the evolution of fiscal policy schools, challenges, historical trajectories, and the ideological shifts that have shaped fiscal policy over time. This chapter also explains the intriguing interplay of politics and fiscal measures.

Chapter Four, The Future of Fiscal Policy: Adapting National Policies to Global Transformations, explores the evolving landscape of national policymaking, emphasizing the need for deliberate policies to promote equity amid challenges. The intricate dance between global economic shifts, public spending in low-income countries, and taxation strategies for development sets the stage for the dynamic future of fiscal policy. Chapter Five: Projections for 2060: Prioritizing Fiscal Reforms for Knowledge-Based Growth projects into the future, addressing global imbalances, uncertain productivity dynamics, the economic impacts of climate change, and how the attendant changes influence the evolution of fiscal policy over time.

Chapter Six: Strategic Structural Reforms for Sustainable Growth and Equity examines the role of national policies in technological advancement and the imperative need for adaptive labor and education policies. Readers are guided through a comprehensive understanding of shaping education policies and transitioning to loan funding models for tertiary education. Lastly, Chapter Seven, Strategic Fiscal and Macroeconomic Policies and Global Economic Shifts takes a panoramic view of the global stage, adapting fiscal instruments to global integration and addressing challenges through structural policy instruments. Overall, the book Fiscal Dynamics in a Transforming Global Economy aims to be a guiding beacon through the intricate web of fiscal policies and economic transformations. It is useful for economists, policymakers, accountants, and avid readers interested in understanding the dynamics shaping our world.

INTRODUCTION

Understanding how fiscal policy is evolving and projecting into the future in a world marked by unprecedented shifts in technology, economics, and global interconnectedness is of immense importance for shaping economic policies now for optimal success. This book serves as a comprehensive guide, unraveling the complexities that define the evolving landscape of public finance and its profound impact on the global economic stage. Our journey begins with exploring the meaning and scope of public finance in Chapter One. From explaining resource allocation to the broader implications of resource allocation, we delve into the core principles that underpin the public sector's role in designing and implementing economic policy and ensuring societal well-being. Chapter One sets the stage, highlighting public finance's vital role in achieving economic stability, equitable resource distribution, and overall societal welfare.

Chapter Two seamlessly transitions into the intersection of public finance and monetary policy. The delicate balance between these two pillars of economic governance is unveiled, offering insights into their collaborative efforts in achieving seamless economic operation. We navigate the characteristics of central banks, the functions of the financial system, and the innovative tools employed to enhance monetary policy, providing readers with a nuanced understanding of this symbiotic relationship.

Chapter Three examines the evolution and challenges of fiscal policy. Drawing from various economic schools and historical trajectories, we examine the constraints and ideological shifts that have shaped fiscal policy over time. This chapter lays bare the intricacies of decision-making, emphasizing the challenges posed by high public debt levels and the pragmatic shifts in economic policies during different eras.

In Chapter Four, we peer into the future, addressing the imperative need for national policies to adapt to global transformations. The chapter underscores the challenges and opportunities with economic growth decelerating and innovation emerging as a cornerstone. The global integration of knowledge-based activities takes center stage, presenting a paradigm shift in traditional redistributive tools and demanding enhanced international policy coordination.

The journey through projections for 2060 unfolds from Chapter Five to Chapter Seven. In Chapter Five, we grapple with the multifaceted challenges post-COVID-19. From fiscal pressures arising from demographic shifts to the uncertainties surrounding future productivity and education dynamics, this chapter projects into a future where strategic fiscal reforms are paramount for knowledge-based growth. Chapter Six looks at strategic structural reforms essential for sustainable growth and equity. As the role of national policies in technological advancement comes under scrutiny, the chapter advocates for adaptive labor and education policies to navigate the complexities of evolving demographics and labor market dynamics.

Our exploration concludes in Chapter Seven, where we widen our lens to examine strategic fiscal and macroeconomic policies amid global economic shifts. From adapting fiscal instruments to global integration to fostering international cooperation in risk-sharing mechanisms, this chapter encapsulates the broader context of fiscal policies in a dynamic, globalized economy.

Fiscal Dynamics in a Transforming Global Economy invites readers to the intricate landscape of fiscal policies shaping our world. This book aims to be a guiding compass for economists, policymakers, and enthusiasts eager to comprehend the forces steering our global economic ship. Join this enlightening journey through fiscal dynamics, where knowledge meets action and global transformations redefine the contours of economic governance.

CHAPTER ONE: EVOLVING DYNAMICS OF PUBLIC FINANCE IN THE DIGITAL ERA

Summary of Key Points

1. Meaning and Scope of Public Finance:

- Public finance explores government actions and policies, examining revenue, expenditures, and debt management.
- The scope includes local, regional, and national analysis, covering revenue collection, resource allocation, and asset/liability management.
- Public finance plays a vital role in shaping economic policy and societal well-being, aiming for economic stability, equitable resource distribution, and overall societal welfare.

2. Objectives of Public Finance:

- Key objectives include Economic stability, equitable income distribution, efficient resource allocation, crisis management, long-term planning, and ensuring fiscal discipline.
- Public finance guides fiscal policies to influence aggregate demand, address market failures, and provide essential public goods and services.
- Its role becomes crucial during crises, fostering global interconnectedness and sustainability in the face of economic, technological, and demo-

graphic changes.

3. Contemporary Issues in Public Finance:

- Globalization and technological advancements impact revenue collection, expenditure management, and financial transparency.
- Public finance shapes national trajectories, requiring a nuanced under-standing of economic principles, political considerations, and global dynamics.
- Managing complexities within public finance involves strategic planning to ensure continued effectiveness.

4. Fiscal Policy:

- Fiscal policy involves government spending and taxation to influence the economy.
- Categorized as expansionary or contractionary, fiscal policy aims to manage aggregate demand and stabilize the economy.
- Effective fiscal policy addresses economic challenges, promotes equity, and ensures long-term sustainability.

5. Foundations of Fiscal Policy:

- Fiscal policy is counter-cyclical, addressing economic cycles through expansionary or contractionary measures.
- It plays a crucial role in providing public goods, promoting equity, and ensuring long-term fiscal sustainability.
- Global interconnectedness influences coordination among nations in managing fiscal policies for economic stability.

6. Public Goods, Market Failures, and Government Failure:

- Public goods pose challenges in market provision, requiring state intervention.

- Market failures, such as monopolies and externalities, necessitate regulatory frameworks within public finances.
- Understanding market and government failures is essential for comprehensive regulatory frameworks and effective public service provision.

Meaning and Scope of Public Finance

Generally, public finance explores the effects of government actions and policies on the economy. Public finance entails scrutinizing government revenue, expenditures, and debt management. According to Dalton (1965), public finance studies the principles governing public authorities' spending and fundraising activities. The scope of public finance involves the dynamic analysis of government activities at various levels—local, regional, and national. It encompasses revenue collection through tax and non-tax avenues, resource allocation through government expenditures, and public assets and liabilities management. This dynamic field evolves in response to economic, political, and technological changes, playing a crucial role in shaping economic policy and influencing societal well-being. Understanding public finance is fundamental for policymakers, economists, and citizens navigating the complexities of economic governance. It revolves around how governments raise funds, allocate resources, and manage financial affairs to achieve economic and social objectives. The overarching goal is to promote economic stability, equitable resource distribution, and overall societal well-being.

The primary source of government revenue is taxation, with various tax systems focusing on income, consumption, property, and other levies. Tax policies aim to balance revenue generation with economic considerations and fairness. Governments also generate income through non-tax means such as fees, fines, and income from state-owned enterprises. The government allocates its expenditure to social programs, infrastructure investment, defense and security, and debt repayment.

1. Social Programs: Public finance allocates healthcare, education, and welfare funds.
2. Infrastructure Investment: Governments invest in building and maintaining infrastructure, a key driver of economic growth. This investment enhances long-term productivity and competitiveness and attracts investments, creating jobs and improving overall productivity.
3. Defense and Security: Allocating resources for national defense and security ensures the safety and sovereignty of the nation.

Public finance equally deals with debt management, which involves examining the government's capacity to borrow funds through issuing bonds and other debt instruments and responsibly managing debt obligations. Debt management involves strategies to ensure the government can meet its financial obligations without compromising fiscal stability.

Objectives of Public Finance

The following are the objectives of public finance:

1. Economic Stability: Public finance aims to achieve economic stability by influencing aggregate demand through fiscal policies, mitigating the impact of recessions and controlling inflation.
2. Equitable Distribution of Income: Progressive taxation and social welfare programs address income inequality, promoting a more equitable distribution of wealth.
3. Resource Allocation: Public finance guides efficient resource allocation to contribute effectively to economic growth and societal welfare, addressing market failures and providing essential public goods and services.
4. Crisis Management: Public finance is crucial during crises, allowing governments to mobilize resources for emergency response efforts and

implement fiscal stimulus measures.

5. Long-Term Planning and Sustainability: Public finance facilitates long-term planning and investment, addressing future challenges like technological advancements, demographic shifts, and environmental sustainability.

6. Ensuring Fiscal Discipline: Through the formulation and execution of government budgets, public finance ensures fiscal discipline and responsible financial management, maintaining transparency and accountability to uphold public trust.

Contemporary Issues in Public Finance

Globalization has underscored countries' need to consider the international implications of their fiscal policies. Concurrently, technological advancements have significantly impacted revenue collection, expenditure management, and financial transparency, with e-government initiatives and digital payment systems becoming integral to modern public finance. As the cornerstone of economic governance, public finance shapes nations' trajectories and their citizens' well-being. Public finance, a linchpin in a nation's economic machinery, profoundly influences economic policy, societal well-being, and sustainable development prospects. Its role in guiding resource allocation, addressing income disparities, and responding to economic challenges makes public finance indispensable for achieving economic stability, growth, and social progress. The complexities within this field necessitate a nuanced understanding of economic principles, political considerations, and the evolving global landscape, making it a dynamic and vital aspect of the broader economic context.

Fiscal Policy

Fiscal policy, involving government spending and taxation to influence the economy, is critical for governments aiming to achieve various economic objectives. Categorized into expansionary or contractionary measures based on economic conditions, fiscal policy historically played a pivotal role during crises, such as the Great Depression in the 1930s. Modern fiscal policy, influenced by economists like John Maynard Keynes, emphasizes government intervention to manage aggregate demand and stabilize the economy. The evolution of fiscal policy unfolds through various economic periods. During wars, increased government spending inadvertently stimulated the economy. Post-World War II saw the establishment of comprehensive welfare states, while recent decades featured debates between fiscal austerity and stimulus advocates. The 2008 global financial crisis highlighted the enduring importance of fiscal policy in contemporary economic management. Taxation, a fundamental component of fiscal policy, serves purposes beyond revenue generation. Taxes fund essential public services and their structure and efficiency impact government revenue. Taxation also plays a vital role in economic stabilization; during expansions, taxes may rise to control inflation, while tax cuts during downturns stimulate economic activity. For instance, during the 2008 financial crisis, governments implemented fiscal measures, including tax cuts and increased public spending, to counter the severe economic downturn. The United States, for instance, introduced the Emergency Economic Stabilization Act and the American Recovery and Reinvestment Act, incorporating tax incentives and spending programs to stimulate economic recovery.

Foundations of Fiscal Policy

As an economic management tool, fiscal policy is built upon several foundational principles and concepts.

Counter-cyclical nature: Primarily, fiscal policy is inherently counter-cyclical, aiming to counteract economic cycles. During downturns, expansionary fiscal policies stimulate demand, while contractionary policies are employed during periods of high inflation. For example, many countries adopted counter-cyclical fiscal policies in response to the 2008 financial crisis. The United States implemented the Troubled Asset Relief Program (TARP) and the American Recovery and Reinvestment Act to inject funds into the economy, preventing a more severe downturn.

Public Goods and Services Provision: Fiscal policy plays a crucial role in providing public goods and services not efficiently produced by the private sector. Through taxation and government spending, fiscal policy ensures the provision of essential services contributing to societal well-being. The Scandinavian Welfare States offer case examples. Scandinavian countries like Sweden, Norway, and Denmark have robust fiscal policies that heavily invest in social welfare programs. High levels of taxation finance comprehensive healthcare, education, and social security systems, contributing to their citizens' high quality of life.

Equity and Redistributive Measures: Another foundation of fiscal policy is its role in promoting equity and addressing income inequality. Progressive taxation and targeted spending programs can redistribute wealth and reduce economic disparities. Progressive Taxation in Europe is a case example. Many European countries employ progressive tax systems, where higher-income individuals pay a higher percentage of their income in taxes. The revenue generated is then used to fund social programs, contributing to a more equitable distribution of resources.

Ensuring Long-Term Fiscal Sustainability: In crafting fiscal policy, it is imperative to consider its long-term sustainability to prevent the accumulation of excessive public debt. Governments must strike a delicate balance between addressing immediate economic challenges and safeguarding the nation's fiscal well-being over the long haul. Japan's Fiscal Challenges offer a pertinent illustration of the necessity for long-term fiscal planning. Confronted with an aging population and a low birth rate, Japan grapples with the imperative of economic stimulus against the backdrop of concerns about escalating public debt. This case underscores the importance of factoring in long-term fiscal sustainability when formulating policies.

Global Interconnectedness: In this era of globalization, fiscal policy is significantly influenced by global economic forces. The actions of one country can reverberate across borders, impacting others. Hence, coordination and cooperation among nations become imperative in managing fiscal policies to foster global economic stability. A notable example of international fiscal collaboration is observed among Eurozone countries. They coordinate their fiscal policies to maintain stability within the currency union. The Stability and Growth Pact establishes guidelines for member states, ensuring the implementation of sound fiscal policies and highlighting the interconnected nature of fiscal decisions in a shared economic space.

Understanding these foundational principles is crucial for policymakers. It enables them to devise effective fiscal policies that address contemporary economic challenges and promote long-term sustainability and equitable development.

Public Finances and the Market Process

Today's modern states operate under a mixed economy, where market mechanisms prevail, but the state actively influences and regulates market conditions. Various economic theories approach the role of the state from different perspectives. The market mechanisms play a pivotal role, with economic activities coordinated by the market without centralized control. Adam Smith's concept of the "invisible hand," introduced in his 1776 book 'The Wealth of Nations,' highlights how the market determines the exchange rate of goods and services, balancing buyers and sellers. Smith emphasized the market's ability to balance private and public interests, suggesting that individual pursuits lead to collective benefits through market mechanisms. However, Smith did not recognize market failures, asserting that government intervention was unnecessary.

Contrary to Smith's view, modern economics acknowledges market failures as a primary reason for state intervention. This recognition gained prominence after the economic crisis 1929, where market imperfections led to severe economic and social issues. Notable examples include the 2008 economic crisis and the current one related to the pandemic. Market failures, indicating conditions that hinder effective market functioning, encompass various aspects:

Failure of Competition: Occurs when a few dominant players, or even a monopoly, control a market segment. Monopolies can arise naturally due to returns to scale or artificially through state legislation.

External Economic Effects (Externalities): Include negative (cost-imposing) and positive (unintended advantage) effects on individuals not participating in economic activities. Environmental pollution is a significant negative externality, prompting state intervention.

Incomplete Markets: Markets rise when supply falls short, such as in insurance and capital markets. Government intervention becomes necessary to address these deficiencies.

Failures of Information: Occur when consumers are harmed due to inadequate information disclosure by private markets. Financial markets exemplify this issue, leading to increased emphasis on financial consumer protection and regulatory measures.

Unemployment, Inflation, Lack of Balance: Constitute macroeconomic problems requiring state intervention. Direct or indirect subsidies to businesses, direct payments to unemployed individuals, and various support services are common measures.

Understanding these market failures is crucial for designing effective public financial regulations. For instance, addressing incomplete markets may involve state coordination to resolve deficiencies, while financial markets may require regulations to ensure consumer protection and fair competition. Unemployment and inflation call for targeted fiscal policies, including subsidies and support services. Recognizing the common good nature of information, especially in financial markets, underscores the need for expansive access to information within society. These considerations are essential for developing a comprehensive regulatory framework within public finances.

Public Goods, Market Failures and Government Failure

The issue of public goods arises because, with state intervention, the market may be able to produce these goods, or at least not in adequate quantities. Public goods serve community consumption, and their use does not exclude others from enjoying them. These goods are products that everyone can use, and no one can be excluded from their use. Two categories of public goods can be identified: 'pure' public goods, where usage incurs no additional cost for others and exclusion is difficult, and 'impure' public goods, where these characteristics apply either partially or not. The consumption of public goods, such as national defense, is uniform for all individuals. However, the 'free rider' problem arises as non-contributors still benefit from these goods, leading the state to enforce contribution through public burden-sharing, achieved through taxes.

Apart from market failures, government failure is recognized in scientific literature as occurring when state intervention fails to achieve its intended purposes. The limitations on the state's influence over the market are attributed to four main reasons: limited information, control restrictions on private market responses, limitations on specialized apparatus, and constraints arising from political processes. Government intervention necessitates extensive information and analysis, and the complex nature of the economy may result in unintended consequences or disadvantages for other market segments. The control of private market responses is limited, and the effectiveness of legislation depends on the prudent and efficient functioning of the specialized apparatus within the government. Additionally, government failures may arise from political processes when decisions impact the entire society but are made by a small group with potential biases towards special interest groups.

The evolving economic role of the state is closely tied to the development of the welfare state and the mixed economy. Different theoretical economic positions exist, with some advocating for an expanded state role while others argue for minimizing it, considering the state itself as a problem. The 21st century witnessed a strengthening of the welfare state, especially after the 2008 crisis, where effective fiscal and monetary policies mitigated its impact. Currently, the state plays a more substantial economic role than ever, extracting a significant portion of the national income to fund public services, which is a unique economic weight compared to other players. The welfare state relies on fundamental rights linked to basic public services, funded by diverse revenues. However, the challenge lies in sustaining economic growth to meet the increasing demands of public services without compromising quality or necessitating excessive tax increases. The literature suggests that the growth of the welfare state may stabilize, prompting a need for strategic planning to ensure its continued effectiveness.

Public Service Provision in the Modern State

The provision of public services in the modern state is intricate, encompassing diverse tasks that have expanded over time, necessitating sufficient public revenues and burden-sharing obligations. The extent of state involvement is measured by the centralization ratio for revenues and the redistribution ratio for expenditures, representing the relationship between state activities and the gross domestic product (GDP). The functions of the modern state are multifaceted and categorized into three aspects in the scientific literature, illustrating the complexity of public responsibilities.

Public Authority Functions: Encompassing defense, state organization, social organization, and jurisdiction.

Welfare Functions: Aimed at reproducing and preserving human capital, with welfare states providing services at varying levels based on economic development and policy.

Economic Policy Functions: Involving roles in economic development, investment promotion, job creation, and managing economic crises.

Execution of Public Tasks

The execution of public tasks involves regulatory, legislative, and financing activities, with laws determining tasks and budgetary management establishing conditions for their provision. The state influences the market economy through fiscal and monetary tools, ensuring economic equilibrium and satisfying public needs. Public tasks encompass a broader concept than state tasks, covering municipal and public body responsibilities and tasks addressing public needs. Legal acts categorize public tasks into four groups: needs that could not be met otherwise, undefined service users, constitutional fundamental rights, and economic state intervention. Public tasks are performed through budgeting bodies within public finances, or the central budget may provide financial coverage for tasks carried out by privately-owned enterprises, non-governmental bodies, or partially state-owned entities. This complexity results in a diverse institutional system, classified based on economic function and public policy sector.

Financing public tasks involves both public and private sources. Private financing includes fee financing, borrowing, and raising capital. User charges under fee financing follow the 'user pays' principle, with different charges enforcing public policy preferences. Borrowing addresses liquidity shortages due to revenue cyclicality, subject to budget deficit and government debt limitations. Raising capital involves private investment in public sector projects through concessions. Primary financing sources in the public sector are the revenues collected by the state through public burden-sharing, forming a dominant funding avenue. This intricate web of tasks, actors, and financing mechanisms underscores the multifaceted nature of public service provision in the modern state.

The Monetarist Foundations of Public Finance

To comprehend the intricacies of finances, one must delve into overarching theoretical aspects regarding money, questioning what qualifies as 'money' and how innovative financial products align with this conceptual framework. Economic theories adopt distinct perspectives on money, some viewing it as a historical category necessitating redefinition due to economic and historical shifts. Before capitalism, a universal form of 'money' encompassing all monetary functions did not exist, evolving with economic development and societal needs. An alternative perspective frames money as an innovation reducing transaction costs, asserting that state approval is unnecessary for it to be considered a valid currency. However, when accepted universally, state recognition becomes pivotal for it to function as commodity money.

The diverse economic concepts related to money need a universally accepted definition, with the functional approach emphasizing money's roles while separating its general currency nature from state approval. Theoretical works identify three fundamental functions of money: exchange, accounting, and value preservation. Money is a general exchange tool, facilitates value measurement in monetary units, and acts as a low-risk value preserver, enabling goods exchange over time. Modern money is illustrated by its dual components: physical cash (currency and coins) and bank account money, represented electronically. In today's economy, credit money, created by banks, plays a determinant role, encompassing trade, payment, and accumulation functions. Theoretical approaches like credit money and endogenous money theory highlight the interplay between money, the banking system, and the central bank.

The creation of modern money only sometimes necessitates state involvement, but regulatory processes encompassing fiscal and monetary policy are imperative. Examining money in legal terms underscores that while economic processes and general acceptance shape money, regulation designates it as a state's official currency through public acts. Money's intricate theoretical foundations involve a dynamic interplay between economic processes, state recognition, and regulatory frameworks, shaping the multifaceted roles money plays in modern finance.

Digitalization and its Impact on Public Finance

Digital financial instruments, encompassing not only cryptocurrencies but also other decentralized services based on digital technologies, play a pivotal role in the evolving landscape of public finance. These instruments, operating through blockchain technology, serve various functions, such as acting as currency (e.g., Bitcoin), infrastructure-securing tools (e.g., Ethereum), and service provision instruments (e.g., Augur). Blockchain, a decentralized database relying on a network, facilitates data storage and movement, relying on the Internet for connectivity. Unlike a centralized network, blockchain employs a distributed network where interconnected computers lack hierarchy, distinguishing it from traditional centralized systems. Cryptographic procedures are critical to the functioning of crypto instruments, ensuring secure transactions without intermediaries. This decentralization feature allows transactions to occur directly between users, reducing costs but simultaneously posing challenges related to state control, including concerns about monetary regulation, money laundering, financial consumer protection, and taxation.

The category of crypto instruments includes cryptocurrencies, with varying perspectives on their nature and characteristics. While the literature often uses 'cryptocurrencies,' a more accurate descriptor would be 'crypto money.' In essence, these digital financial instruments serve as general value measures, exchange tools, and electronic means of payment. From a legal perspective, cryptocurrencies still need to be developed in many countries. Central banks commonly have found it difficult to recognize cryptocurrencies as legal tenders, although their common use by the populace needs to be improved. For instance, the Hungarian National Bank (MNB) expresses concerns about the risks associated with cryptocurrencies, emphasizing their lack of supervision and regulation compared to traditional financial solutions. MNB underscores the risks of purchasing cryptocurrencies, emphasizing potential issues such as availability concerns and susceptibility to digital theft through hacking. The absence of consumer protection, liability rules, and compensation mechanisms further complicates the landscape, placing the burden of potential damages solely on the individual consumer.

While these concerns highlight genuine problems, it is crucial to note that similar risks exist in regulated markets with traditional financial instruments. However, the comparison changes when juxtaposing cryptocurrencies with official currencies. MNB's warning gains relevance from the perspective of traditional currency standards, but when viewed as financial instruments, the concerns raised hold partial validity. Investors must be mindful that the cryptocurrency market needs more regulation, and the safeguards offered by regulated markets, including law enforcement, consumer protection, and supervisory mechanisms, are absent. Recognizing these digital assets' unique risks and benefits is crucial for navigating the evolving landscape of financial instruments in the digital era.

Review Questions

1. What are the key objectives of public finance, and how does it contribute to economic stability?
2. Explain the counter-cyclical nature of fiscal policy and its role in addressing economic challenges.
3. How do market failures necessitate state intervention, and what are the common types of market failures?
4. Discuss the foundations of fiscal policy, emphasizing its role in promoting equity and long-term sustainability.
5. How does globalization influence the coordination of fiscal policies among nations for economic stability?
6. Evaluate the challenges and benefits of digitalizing financial instruments in public finance.

Discussion Points

1. Explore the role of public finance in addressing contemporary challenges such as technological advancements and globalization.
2. Discuss the potential impact of digital financial instruments, including cryptocurrencies, on traditional public finance structures and regulations.
3. Analyze the evolving dynamics of fiscal policy in response to global economic changes and the importance of international cooperation in managing fiscal policies.

CHAPTER TWO: THE INTERSECTION OF PUBLIC FINANCE AND MONETARY POLICY

Summary of Key Points

1. Interplay of Public Finance and Monetary Policy:

- Seamless economic operation depends on the intricate relationship between public finance and monetary policy, jointly managed by the state and central bank.
- Monetary policy, characterized by independence, impacts economic sectors through the expansion or restriction of money supply and credit.

2. Functions of the Financial System:

- Financial intermediaries operating in markets like capital and insurance connect savers to investors and play a vital role in the financial system.
- The financial system serves functions such as resource reallocation, risk management, fundraising, and acting as a clearinghouse for swift transaction handling.

3. Roles and Characteristics of Central Banks:

- Central banks, pivotal in the monetary system, maintain independence through operational, institutional, personal, and financial autonomy.
- They serve as the bank of the state, the bank of the banks, and the ultimate lender, supporting the government's economic policy without compromising primary goals.

4. Enhancements in Monetary Policy:

- Microprudential and macroprudential supervision are vital for overseeing specific financial intermediaries and mitigating risks.
- Complemented by innovative tools like securities purchase programs, interest rate reduction enhances financial market liquidity.

5. Liquidity Enhancement by Central Banks:

- Central banks employ diverse tools to enhance liquidity, including expanded collateral scope, long-term loans, and adjustments to interest rate corridors.
- Ongoing risks such as operational challenges, state-ordered loan repayment moratoriums, and increased cyber threats impact the banking sector.

6. Fiscal Policy and Economic Development:

- Fiscal policy's macroeconomic impact in developing countries requires prudent management of budget deficits and public debt levels.
- The microeconomic perspective emphasizes the need for efficient and targeted government expenditure to drive human development, especially in education and health.

The seamless operation of today's economy hinges on the intricate interplay between public finance and monetary policy, with regulation managed jointly by the state and the central bank. Monetary policy, aimed at achieving the primary goals of fiscal policy while maintaining autonomy, is characterized by its independence from the government. This autonomy is guaranteed through the central bank's independence and accountability to the state's legislative body. Monetary policy employs flexible measures that selectively impact economic sectors through monetary expansion or restriction. Monetary expansion generally increases money supply and credit, fostering higher output, increased demand, and employment growth.

Conversely, monetary restriction entails a general tightening of money supply and credit, deterring economic growth. The effectiveness of monetary policy in influencing financial processes and the economy in the short or medium term relies on specific tools. These tools encompass reserve rules, refinancing, interest rate regulation, securities operations, exchange rate policy, and other central bank assets.

The financial system functions as the economy's circulatory system, facilitating the flow of financial resources from savers to investors. Financial intermediaries play a crucial role in connecting financial resources to users in national and international markets, operating within the financial, capital, and insurance markets. These markets are closely intertwined through financial intermediaries, often operating as financial conglomerates, posing regulatory challenges. Regulation of the financial system involves public and private law, with public law governing institutionalization, control, supervision, establishment, termination, and operation.

The modern financial system serves various functions, including the reallocation of resources, risk management, fundraising and distribution, and a clearinghouse function. It enables the concentration of funds for large investments, reduces individual risks through risk management tools like insurance, and allows small investors to participate in diverse investments through investment funds. Under the clearinghouse function, the financial system ensures swift money flow through transaction handling. Digitalization has expedited and reduced the cost of financial transactions in the market. The financial system manages a diverse array of financial tools, such as money, bank deposits, credit market instruments, shares, units of financial markets, investment funds, pension contributions, and financial derivatives.

The central institution in the monetary system is the central bank. However, within the Eurozone, the independence of monetary policy has shifted to the European System of Central Banks and the European Central Bank. While central banks support fiscal policy, they maintain independence in formulating monetary policy, characterized by operational, institutional, personal, and financial independence. Operational independence ensures autonomy from the government and institutional independence guards against government influence on policy formulation. Personal independence prevents undue influence, while financial independence ensures the central bank's autonomy in funding its operations.

Roles and Characteristics of Central Banks

Central banks, as pivotal institutions in the monetary system, exhibit distinctive features and functions that contribute to the overall stability and functioning of the economy.

Independence Criteria: Personal independence dictates that the decision-making bodies of central banks should not be subject to instructions from EU institutions, state governments, or their respective organs while executing their duties. Financial independence is a separate criterion ensuring that central banks possess sufficient financial resources for executing tasks, as evidenced by substantial funds and the ability to define their management independently.

Monetary Policy Objectives: Central banks are characterized by the objectives guiding their monetary policies. Three prevalent forms include a complex system of objectives encompassing economic stability with sub-goals like growth, low inflation, and low unemployment. In inflation target-tracking, central banks aim to maintain low but positive inflation through monetary policy tools. Alternatively, exchange rate target-tracking is employed when a country maintains a fixed exchange rate, wherein the central bank aligns its monetary policy to achieve the predetermined exchange rate.

Central Bank Functions: Central banks serve various roles within the banking system. They are the state's bank, managing official currency issuance and holding foreign and gold reserves. The state usually has a majority stake in the central bank, and, as the bank of the state, it supports the government's economic policy without compromising its primary goals. This collaborative regulation emphasizes the importance of consistency in fiscal and monetary policies. In the role of the bank of the banks, central banks maintain accounts for credit institutions, influence lending and liquidity, and regulate overall banking system operations. As the ultimate lender, they provide exceptional credit to banks facing liquidity challenges.

Supervisory Functions: Central banks embraced macroprudential supervision after the 2008 economic crisis, which involves identifying and mitigating risks to the financial intermediary system, preventing the emergence and spread of risks that could threaten stability.

Enhancements in Monetary Policy

Microprudential supervision: This is an optional function carried out by either the central bank or a distinct supervisory body and plays a crucial role in overseeing specific members of the financial intermediary system and individual organizations. This supervision ensures compliance with regulatory standards, ultimately safeguarding financial stability. An illustrative example of effective monetary policy operation is evident in the response to the economic crisis triggered by the recent pandemic. Central banks utilized various instruments to implement monetary policy, influencing the supply and demand for money and credit. While traditional central bank instruments were once considered sufficient, the aftermath of the previous economic crisis prompted leading central banks worldwide to adopt new elements in their toolkit, intensifying their role in managing economic crises.

Interest rate reduction: This conventional instrument proved less effective when rates dipped below zero. Consequently, central banks introduced innovative tools, such as securities purchase programs, to enhance financial market liquidity. For instance, the European Central Bank incorporated corporate credit claims as coverage during the 2008 economic crisis. This strategy persisted as a crucial tool in the Eurozone's monetary policy post-crisis. Central banks' toolkit has expanded in terms of volume and response to the ongoing crisis. For example, the Federal Reserve System, known as 'the Fed,' responded swiftly to the economic downturn by reducing interest rates and implementing quantitative easing without a financial envelope. The Fed engaged in the purchase of government annuities, real estate-based mortgages, and corporate annuities. Similarly, the Hungarian National Bank adjusted its monetary policy toolkit to address the impacts of the COVID-19 crisis, outlining specific objectives and the instruments allocated.

The Hungarian National Bank, for instance, classified its tools into three key areas based on objectives: ensuring liquidity, shaping short-term yields more flexibly, and influencing long-term yields. To enhance liquidity, the central bank expanded the scope of eligible collaterals, including corporate loans as collateral, enabling large corporations' claims exceeding one billion forints to be included. Investment funds gained access to central bank resources, allowing them to borrow with unit coverage. A long-term central bank loan facility was also introduced to ease financial market tensions. To ensure flexibility in short-term yields, the central bank reintroduced the one-week deposit tool, symmetrically adjusted the interest rate corridor, and anchored the base rate at the middle of the corridor. This adjustment provided the necessary flexibility for effective monetary transmission.

Enhancing Liquidity: In pursuing increased liquidity, the central bank has implemented measures that impact long-term yields. The Funding for Growth Scheme underwent restructuring alongside the launch of a new program, Funding for Growth Scheme Go!, aiming to expand domestic business financing further. While these initiatives present advantageous financing options, it remains to be seen whether they will bring entirely new liquidity or merely lead to the replacement of existing loans by companies. Modifications to the Funding for Growth Scheme included relaxed conditions, increasing exposure to a company group to 50 million forints, and extending the validity of bonds to 20 years. Long-term credit instruments and the asset purchase program were introduced, allowing the central bank to purchase government annuities and mortgage bonds. The latter program remains open-ended, continuing as long as the economic crisis necessitates. The mortgage bond purchase program involves acquiring fixed-rate mortgage bonds issued in forints, traded on the Budapest Stock Exchange, with a minimum remaining validity of one year.

Beyond traditional monetary policy instruments, the central bank employs additional tools to enhance liquidity, aligning with major central banks and playing a pivotal role in the financial market. The ongoing crisis has significantly impacted the banking system, with increasing risks to financial institutions. While the banking system demonstrated better preparedness due to strong regulation during the 2008 crisis, risks persist at individual and systemic levels. Operational risks have evolved with emerging risk factors related to the pandemic, including the heightened importance of geopolitical risk and the resilience of enterprises in restoring operations post-crisis. The risk of outsourcing, potential remote work disruptions, and increased internal and external fraud and cyber-attacks are notable concerns.

The state-ordered loan repayment moratorium further influences the banking sector, allowing companies and households to extend their loans, increasing liquidity and aiding business operations. Maximizing the total cost of credit ratio for consumer loans also affects households' economic well-being. These evolving risks provide an opportunity for legislative adjustments based on experience, particularly as the world faces the uncertainties of potential future pandemics. Drawing lessons from the current crisis offers a valuable opportunity for further scientific research and the re-regulation of specific areas.

Fiscal Policy and Economic Development

Fiscal policy fosters growth and human development, operating through various macroeconomic and microeconomic channels. However, insights from research conducted in industrialized countries and developing nations raise questions about its efficacy in diverse contexts.

Firstly, from a macroeconomic perspective, past research emphasizes the significance of prudent fiscal policy in developing countries, marked by low budget deficits and public debt levels. Such policies are essential for sustained economic growth, poverty reduction, and improved social outcomes. Small budget deficits mitigate the risk of economic crises, ensuring stability and leading to higher investment, growth, and educational attainment. Traditionally, economists advocate for countercyclical fiscal policy to address short-term fluctuations in output and employment. However, there is a growing recognition that in certain circumstances, particularly when public debt is high and unsustainable, expansionary budgets may yield different positive effects. Reductions in budget deficits, under such conditions, are found to accelerate growth by lowering interest rates, catalyzing private investment, and stimulating private consumption.

Secondly, from the microeconomics perspective, taxes impact private agents' decisions to save and invest, potentially altering the growth rate. However, empirical evidence on the direct impact of taxes on growth remains inconclusive, partly due to simultaneous expenditure policies. Endogenous growth theory suggests that increased spending on education, health, infras-tructure, and research can boost long-term growth, generating resources to further invest in human capital. However, economists agree that public expenditure affects growth and directly influences human development outcomes, particularly in the context of Sustainable Development Goals (SDGs). Government expenditure policies can play a pivotal role in achieving SDGs by focusing on education and health outcomes. However, more than the spending level matters, the efficiency and targeting of expenditures, especially towards low-income people, are crucial.

Thirdly, on the financing side, the relationship between external debt and economic activity is complex. While foreign borrowing can positively impact investment and growth up to a certain threshold, high-interest bills on debt may constrain productive spending. The debate on aid's impact on growth in developing countries is ongoing, with varying research outcomes. As the International Monetary Fund (IMF) is deeply invested in fiscal issues, understanding the dynamics of fiscal policy, growth, and poverty in developing countries remains a key focus. Research in this realm has evolved, emphasizing the need for context-specific insights and highlighting the intricate relationship between fiscal policy and development outcomes. However, critics of the IMF contend that the recommendation for fiscal adjustment, even when fiscal problems are not the root cause of macroeconomic imbalances, overlooks the potential adverse consequences of fiscal retrenchment. An alternative approach involving a relaxation of fiscal policy might be more suitable, particularly for countries grappling with significant output losses during crises. A key concern in this debate revolves around the implications of changes in fiscal stance on growth.

Fourthly, when countries exhibit high public debt levels and borrowing costs, empirical evidence suggests that fiscal consolidation can enhance growth by bolstering market confidence, improving market access for private and public borrowers, and reducing interest rates. Even for countries lacking market access, fiscal consolidation can spur growth, especially if accompanied by structural reforms fostering labor market flexibility and enhanced factor productivity. Existing empirical research, mainly focused on industrialized countries, explores the conditions under which fiscal consolidation leads to stable or increased output. Studies, such as Giavazzi and Pagano (1990), indicate that consolidations tend to be expansionary when debt is high or escalating. They argue that private spending positively responds to a credible commitment to debt reduction and a reduction in the risk premium.

Additionally, research by Alesina and Perotti (1995) and Alesina and Ardagna (1998) underscores the role of budget composition in explaining diverse private sector responses to fiscal policy and, consequently, its impact on growth. Fiscal adjustments emphasizing cuts in transfers and the wage bill tend to be longer-lasting and potentially expansionary. In contrast, those relying on tax increases and public investment cuts tend to be contractionary and unsustainable.

However, the literature needs an in-depth exploration of the relevance of these concerns for developing countries, particularly low-income nations. Questions arise: Is a smaller budget deficit conducive to growth? Should developing countries curtail public spending, especially those anticipating substantial increases in aid inflows? Given their specific institutional features, limited evidence exists on the short-term effects of countercyclical fiscal policy in developing countries. Financing constraints, especially in countries lacking access to international capital markets, can lead to strong crowding-out and inflationary effects when the fiscal deficit exceeds manageable levels. Simultaneously, the relatively high marginal propensity to consume may amplify the size of the fiscal multiplier. This debate gains significance as some argue that fiscal policy in IMF-supported programs is overly stringent, impeding economic growth in developing countries pursuing fiscal austerity. Addressing three core empirical questions becomes imperative:

1. How do fiscal stance, expenditure composition, and budget financing impact economic growth in developing countries?
2. How do these factors, along with others, influence the persistence of fiscal adjustments?
3. Through which channels does fiscal consolidation exert its impact on growth?

Enhancing Growth through Fiscal Adjustment: Insights for Developing Countries

Fiscal adjustment emerges as a potential catalyst for growth in low-income countries grappling with macroeconomic imbalances. Research indicates that channeling a larger portion of public spending into public investment stimulates economic growth. Notably, pruning specific current expenditures yields higher growth rates compared to adjustments based on revenue hikes and cuts in more productive spending—an outcome consistent with findings in industrialized countries. Particularly, fiscal consolidations that curtail domestic financing of the deficit stand out as the most pro-growth. Conversely, expanding selected current expenditures aligns with higher growth in countries achieving macroeconomic stability with low budget deficits and inflation rates.

While fiscal adjustments occur in some countries, their transient nature often hinders a positive impact on growth. Scholars agree that persistent fiscal consolidation is essential to maximize its growth effects. Hence, a crucial question arises: What factors determine the duration of a fiscal adjustment program? Baldacci, Clements, Gupta, and Mulas-Granados's assessment shows that the protection of capital expenditure during fiscal adjustment emerges as a key factor in prolonging the episode. Likewise, an increased share of current spending on non-wage goods and services contributes to a longer fiscal consolidation. Additionally, a reinforced revenue effort tends to sustain adjustment, while expenditure reductions play a secondary role. This finding contrasts with industrialized countries, where literature emphasizes that sustained fiscal adjustment hinges on expenditure reductions.

Another pertinent aspect is understanding the channels through which fiscal consolidation influences growth in developing countries and whether they differ from those in industrialized nations. In industrial countries, the primary channel involves increased growth through higher private investment following reduced real interest rates, improved price stability, and enhanced external stability. However, Baldacci, Hillman, and Kojo propose that fiscal adjustment in developing countries primarily stimulates growth through its impact on factor productivity. The investment channel is less critical due to the low productivity of public spending in countries grappling with weak governance. Notably, changes in spending composition that elevate the share of public-sector wages and salaries while reducing capital spending tend to impede growth associated with rent-seeking behavior. Additionally, experts suggest that fiscal contractions reducing borrowing from domestic sources are most conducive to growth.

Fiscal Adjustment in Developing Countries

In pursuing economic growth, fiscal adjustment emerges as a pivotal force, especially for low-income countries with macroeconomic imbalances. The research underscores the potency of directing a significant portion of public spending toward public investment to fuel economic growth. Notably, trimming specific current expenditures proves more effective in boosting growth rates compared to adjusting through revenue hikes or cuts in more productive spending—an observation consistent with findings in industrial-ized nations. Fiscal consolidations that trim domestic deficit financing are highlighted as the most growth-oriented. Conversely, expanding selected cur-rent expenditures correlates with heightened growth in countries achieving macroeconomic stability with low budget deficits and inflation rates.

While fiscal adjustments manifest in some countries, their fleeting impact often impedes positive growth outcomes. Scholars agree that sustained fiscal consolidation is imperative for optimizing growth effects; this prompts a crucial inquiry: What factors influence the duration of a fiscal adjustment program? According to an evaluation by Baldacci, Clements, Gupta, and Mulas-Granados, safeguarding capital expenditure during fiscal adjustment emerges as a key factor prolonging the adjustment episode. Similarly, an increased allocation of current spending on non-wage goods and services contributes to a more prolonged fiscal consolidation. Furthermore, a strengthened revenue effort tends to sustain adjustment, while reductions in expenditure play a secondary role. This finding diverges from industrialized countries, where literature underscores the centrality of expenditure reductions for persistent fiscal adjustment.

Another critical consideration involves discerning the channels through which fiscal consolidation shapes growth in developing countries and whether these mechanisms differ from those in industrialized nations. While industrial countries primarily experience increased growth through higher private investment following reduced real interest rates and enhanced stability, Baldacci, Hillman, and Kojo argue that fiscal adjustment in developing countries predominantly stimulates growth by impacting factor productivity.

The investment channel holds less significance due to the low productivity of public spending in countries grappling with weak governance. Notably, alterations in spending composition that elevate the share of public-sector wages and salaries while reducing capital spending tend to hinder pro-growth, which is linked with rent-seeking behavior. Experts also suggest that fiscal contractions reducing domestic borrowing are conducive to growth.

Fiscal Rules and Budgetary Convergence in WAEMU: Lessons and Challenges

The strategic use of fiscal policy plays a crucial role in fostering short- and long-term economic growth. Many countries have implemented fiscal rules to facilitate fiscal consolidation and ensure fiscal sustainability. A study conducted by Doré and Masson on fiscal stability within the West African Economic and Monetary Union (WAEMU) sheds light on the impact of cyclical variations and terms-of-trade fluctuations on the convergence criteria (fiscal rules) applied since 1999. The establishment of budgetary rules was rooted in the belief that fiscal consolidation would unleash resources for the private sector, paving the way for sustainable growth. Despite significant progress, the WAEMU's experience has yielded mixed results, especially after the 1994 devaluation. Initial strides in robust growth and fiscal consolidation were followed by a notable deterioration in the fiscal balance across most countries after 1997. While adverse terms-of-trade developments undeniably contributed to negative impacts on growth and budget deficits, several countries experienced fiscal slippages primarily due to weakened economic policies, which impeded robust and sustained growth within the Union.

The analysis underscores the importance of governments focusing on specific measures to meet fiscal convergence standards. It emphasizes the need to reduce the proportion of public wages and vigilantly monitor other current operating expenditures. In pursuing fiscal adjustments, the limited room for reducing overall expenditure while addressing poverty concerns calls for a shift towards enhancing the quality of fiscal adjustments and fortifying tax efforts, entailing optimizing expenditure structures, such as more efficient deployment of civil service staff and sustained efforts to boost revenue. The study thus advocates for a nuanced approach that considers fiscal quantity and places equal emphasis on fiscal quality and revenue enhancement in pursuing fiscal convergence and sustainable growth within the WAEMU.

Review Questions

1. How does the independence of central banks contribute to the effectiveness of monetary policy?
2. What are the key functions of financial intermediaries in the financial system, and how do they connect savers to investors?
3. Explain the roles of central banks as the bank of the state, the bank of the banks, and the ultimate lender.
4. How have central banks adapted their monetary policy toolkit in response to recent economic crises?
5. What risks are associated with liquidity enhancements by central banks, especially in the context of evolving operational challenges?
6. Discuss the macroeconomic and microeconomic considerations for the efficacy of fiscal policy in promoting economic growth in developing countries.

Discussion Points

1. Explore the implications of shifting monetary policy independence to the Eurozone's European System of Central Banks. How does this impact the autonomy of individual central banks?
2. Assess the effectiveness of unconventional monetary policy tools, such as securities purchase programs, in addressing liquidity challenges. What are the potential risks associated with these measures?

3. Discuss the challenges and opportunities in aligning fiscal policy with sustainable development goals (SDGs) and the role of government expenditure in achieving positive outcomes.

CHAPTER THREE: EVOLUTION AND CHALLENGES OF FISCAL POLICY

Summary of Key Points

1. Evolution of Fiscal Policy Schools:

  - Fiscal policy has evolved, incorporating insights from various economic schools such as classical economics, Keynesian economics, and modern monetary theory (MMT).
  - Monetarists and supply-side economists challenged the effectiveness of fiscal policy, emphasizing the role of monetary policy.
  - Shifts in economic policies during the 1970s and 1980s reduced reliance on active fiscal policy.

2. Challenges and Constraints:

  - Fiscal policy effectiveness is constrained by fiscal space, the government's capacity to use fiscal measures without compromising fiscal sustainability.
  - High public debt levels can limit the ability to implement expansionary fiscal policies.
  - Inherent time lags in decision-making and policy impact pose challenges in responding promptly to economic changes.

3. Historical Trajectory and Ideological Shifts:

- The historical trajectory reflects the ebb and flow of Keynesian ideas, with dominance during the Kennedy administration giving way to challenges and shifts.
- The delayed 1968 tax surcharge and its perceived failure tarnished Keynesianism, suggesting limitations in controlling demand.

4. Pragmatic Shift in Economic Policy:

- Policymakers, even those initially hostile to Keynesianism, tend to adopt Keynesian measures during recessions, as seen in the 2001 and 2008-2009 responses.
- The global financial crisis led to a widespread return to Keynesian policies, with nations implementing fiscal stimuli to address aggregate demand shortages.

5. Political Patterns and Fiscal Policy:

- Political patterns show a tendency for Republicans to criticize deficits under Democratic leadership but embrace them under Republican rule.
- The pandemic altered the deficit narrative in 2020, with bipartisan support for fiscal measures, reflecting a pragmatic embrace of Keynesian measures.

6. Central Bank Independence (CBI) Evolution:

- The stance on Central Bank Independence (CBI) has evolved since 1961, with a shift towards independence, particularly influenced by the inflationary experiences of the 1970s and 1980s.
- Recent collaborations between the Federal Reserve and the Treasury during crises raise questions about the boundaries of traditional central bank roles.

Fiscal policy is evolving, incorporating insights from various economic schools. Monetarists and supply-side economists questioned fiscal policy's effectiveness, emphasizing the role of monetary policy. The 1970s and 1980s witnessed a shift towards conservative economic policies, reducing reliance on active fiscal policy. Despite debates about its optimal use, effectiveness, and limitations, fiscal policy remains crucial, especially during major economic crises. The effectiveness of fiscal policy is constrained by fiscal space, the government's capacity to use fiscal measures without compromising fiscal sustainability. High public debt levels can limit the ability to implement expansionary fiscal policies. Inherent time lags in decision-making and policy impact pose challenges in responding promptly to economic changes. The historical trajectory of fiscal versus monetary policy reflects real-world events and the ebb and flow of Keynesian ideas, particularly in fiscal policy. Keynesian dominance in Washington's thinking during the Kennedy administration and the Kennedy-Johnson tax cuts was followed by shifting sands in both intellectual and policy arenas. The delayed 1968 tax surcharge and apparent failure tarnished Keynesianism, suggesting that fiscal policy might be effective in boosting demand but less reliable in reining it.

Historical Evolution of Fiscal Policy

Classical Economic Theories: Dating back to economists like Adam Smith and David Ricardo, classical economic theories underline the efficiency of free markets and advocate for a limited government role in economic affairs. Adam Smith's "Wealth of Nations" argued that individuals, driven by self-interest in a free market, inadvertently contribute to overall economic well-being through the "invisible hand" of the market, eliminating the need for government intervention.

Keynesian Economics: Developed by John Maynard Keynes in response to the Great Depression, Keynesian economics calls for active government involvement to manage aggregate demand and stabilize economic fluctuations. Keynes proposed that during economic downturns, the government should increase spending and reduce taxes to stimulate economic activity, marking a departure from classical thought, which relied on market self-correction.

Post-World War II Era: The post-World War II era witnessed the widespread adoption of Keynesian principles in economic policymaking. Governments globally actively used fiscal policy to manage demand, employment, and inflation, addressing challenges from the Great Depression to post-war reconstruction and growth.

Modern Monetary Theory (MMT): Modern Monetary Theory challenges conventional views on government spending and deficits. Advocates argue that governments with sovereign control over their currency can issue money for spending without relying heavily on taxation. MMT suggests that as long as government spending does not lead to excessive inflation, fiscal capacity allows funding of public services without adhering to traditional budgetary balance notions. The intellectual landscape witnessed the seeds of monetarism sprouting with Friedman and Schwartz's influential work. Monetarism gained traction in the 1960s, fueled by Friedman's influence and a surge in inflation that monetarists attributed to Keynesian policies. The 1970s and early 1980s saw another boost for monetarism as supply shocks hit, even though inflation soared for reasons unrelated to money supply.

Shifts in Fiscal Policy Perception: The delayed passage and perceived failure of the 1968 tax surcharge had profound effects. Firstly, it dimmed the appeal of Keynesianism. Secondly, fiscal policy might more effectively boost demand than curbing it. The responsibility for fighting inflation would now rest primarily with the Federal Reserve.

Challenges to Keynesian Theory: The stagflation of the 1970s opened doors to "new classical" economics, often termed the "rational expectations revolution." This approach, challenging Keynesian theory, asserted that markets clear quickly, rendering monetary policy effective only with surprises under rational expectations. While it gained academic traction, it faced skepticism from central bankers who saw real-world impacts of tight monetary policies in the U.K. under Margaret Thatcher and in the U.S. under Paul Volcker.

Monetarism in Policy Circles: In the policy arena, Keynesianism declined as monetarism rose, leading to the Fed's alleged conversion to monetarism in 1979. However, wild fluctuations in money demand and accompanying gyrations in money growth and interest rates dealt a blow to monetarism's credibility.

Reaganomics and Fiscal Policy Focus: Ronald Reagan's use of Keynesian tax cuts as "supply-side" measures marked the last significant reliance on fiscal policy as a macro stabilizer. Reaganomics left chronic deficits, making deficit reduction the new fiscal focus. This trend continued through the 1990 budget agreement under President George H. W. Bush.

Clintonomics and the Anti-Keynesian Era: Under the Clinton presidency, the focus shifted to reducing the federal budget deficit, challenging Keynesian notions. Clintonomics' success prompted anti-Keynesian thoughts, such as negative fiscal multipliers. The period raised questions about whether fiscal policy, through credible deficit reduction promises, could stimulate the economy.

The shift in Economic Policy Debate (2000-2001): The economic policy debate during the 2000 presidential election centered on the federal government's surpluses. Bush advocated for a supply-side tax cut, while Gore aimed to reduce the national debt. Neither position aligned with Keynesian rhetoric. Throughout the period from 1982 to 2001, economists predominantly prioritized monetary policy over fiscal considerations.

Academic Revival of Keynesianism: In the academic realm, Keynesians faced challenges from monetarism, supply-side economics, new classical economics, and real business cycle theory. However, academic trends began to shift back toward Keynesianism in the late 1990s, as proponents of new classical economics acknowledged that macro markets do not clear instantly, endorsing Keynesian policy implications even under rational expectations.

From Principle to Practice: The Pragmatic Shift in Economic Policy

In economic policy, the phrase "no atheists in foxholes" finds resonance, highlighting how policymakers, even those ostensibly hostile to Keynesianism, tend to adopt Keynesian measures when faced with a recession. A prime example unfolded in 2001 when George W. Bush, an advocate of supply-side tax cuts, pivoted to fiscal stimulus, recognizing the need during an economic downturn. Although not self-proclaimed as a Keynesian, Alan Greenspan also embraced Keynesian principles by cutting the federal funds rate through the Federal Reserve, which, however, was merely a prelude to the larger Keynesian turn triggered by the global financial crisis, culminating in the Great Recession of 2007-9. Policymakers worldwide swiftly embraced Keynesian policies, tacitly acknowledging the urgency to address the common problem of an aggregate demand shortage. International summit meetings in 2008 and 2009 showcased this global shift towards Keynesianism, with nations pursuing their self-interests to boost aggregate demand. Notably, even "communist" China took the lead with a substantial fiscal stimulus, followed by the United States under President Obama.

Despite the initial cooperation, the romance with Keynesianism waned. In the United States, a Republican-dominated Congress reverted to concerns about the budget deficit, leading to contractionary fiscal policies from 2011 to 2013, against the preferences of both President Obama and Fed Chair Bernanke. The fiscal cliff scares in 2013 epitomized this policy shift. The déjà vu moment recurred with Donald Trump's presidency in 2017. The context differed while Trump's tax cuts mirrored those of George W. Bush. Trump's tax cuts, amid low unemployment, were enacted with an existing budget deficit, and his supply-side rhetoric set ambitious growth targets. The claims were met with scepticism from serious economists.

The 2017 tax cuts left the federal budget imbalanced, and when the pandemic struck in 2020, a familiar Keynesian response unfolded globally. The Federal Reserve slashed interest rates, and Congress swiftly passed the monumental CARES Act in March 2020, followed by additional fiscal relief in December 2020 and March 2021. The extensive fiscal response to COVID-19 drew parallels with the mobilization efforts during World War II, underscoring the pragmatic embrace of Keynesian measures when economic challenges demand swift and substantial intervention.

Shifting Tides: The Ever-Evolving Landscape of Fiscal Policy

President Eisenhower would have dismissed "Do deficits matter?" as trivial. In the 1950s, deficits were perceived as inflationary, even without Fed monetization, though the precise mechanism remained unclear. Keynesianism, facing criticism for seemingly endorsing budget deficits, received a blow. Surveying 60 years of fiscal policy, 2021 exhibited more Keynesian leanings than 1961. However, the journey was fraught with bumps and political nuances. Classifying American presidents based on their approach to fiscal policy, Kennedy, Johnson, Nixon, Ford, Carter, Obama, and Biden were unequivocally Keynesians, both in principle and practice. While disavowing the Keynesian label, Reagan, Bush II, and Trump acted in a Keynesian manner. The only anti-Keynesian episodes transpired under Bush I and Clinton, where deficit reduction took precedence.

Leaders of monetary policy, from William McChesney Martin to Jerome Powell, were easier to categorize. Few wished to be labeled Keynesians, but their aggregate demand management aligned with Keynesian principles. Examining attitudes toward deficits and national debt over six decades reveals significant shifts. In the 1950s, deficits were deemed fiscally imprudent, morally repugnant, and inflationary, with alleged adverse impacts on future generations. The Kennedy-Johnson era marked a departure as taxes were cut despite existing deficits. The focus shifted to deficits burdening future generations by crowding out investment. The Reagan era, paradoxically, witnessed a surge in deficits, challenging the balanced budget ideology. Supply-side proponents envisioned budget balancing; a vision that needed to be fulfilled. The subsequent 15 years fixated on deficit reduction, exemplified by the pay-as-you-go system. George W. Bush swiftly overturned this trend, abandoning fiscal discipline with tax cuts, wars, and new entitlement programs, turning surpluses into deficits.

A discernible political pattern emerged: Republicans criticized deficits under Democratic leadership but embraced them under Republican rule, particularly with tax cuts benefiting the affluent. Barack Obama faced limitations in pursuing fiscal stimulus post-2009. The frugal approach persisted under the next Republican president, Trump, whose tax cuts were unfunded. The pandemic altered the deficit narrative in 2020. Both parties united to mobilize fiscal policy, overlooking deficit concerns. The CARES Act witnessed bipartisan support. However, as the CARES Act funds waned, a partisan debate erupted over subsequent relief packages, revealing deep divides over deficit concerns. The journey through fiscal policy's twists and turns reflects a dynamic interplay of economic theories, political ideologies, and responses to crises, underscoring the complexity of managing deficits over time.

President Biden's Fiscal Maneuvers and the Evolution of Central Bank Independence

President Joe Biden, armed with narrow majorities in both Congressional chambers, orchestrated the passage of another substantial Covid relief bill in March 2021. Despite the razor-thin majorities, Biden secured the enactment of a sizable budget-altering relief package, including additional relief checks. Notably, the votes in both chambers strictly followed party lines, resulting in a 50-50 tie in the Senate, ultimately broken by Vice President Harris. The Republicans raised concerns, citing the ballooning national debt, which reached 96 per cent of GDP by the close of fiscal 2021, which marked a full-circle journey from a balanced budget in fiscal 1960 to a deficit exceeding 12 per cent of GDP in 2021. Subsequently, Biden and the Democrats encountered challenges in advancing additional spending initiatives. Although a bipartisan infrastructure bill exceeding $1 trillion did pass in 2021, it, at least, carried the semblance of being financially supported.

The Ascent of Central Bank Independence (CBI)

A significant yet often overlooked transformation in the monetary-fiscal domain since 1961 has been the evolving stance on central bank independence (CBI). Initially, CBI was not widely embraced, even in the United States, where the Federal Reserve's independence was atypical globally. Notable economists, including James Tobin and Milton Friedman, questioned the wisdom of CBI. The Nixon era witnessed a low point for CBI when the president sought substantial influence over monetary policy, a sentiment seemingly accepted by Fed Chair Arthur Burns. The landscape shifted dramatically with Paul Volcker at the helm of the Fed. Unyielding in his independence, Volcker steered an aggressive anti-inflation course during a deep recession. The inflationary experiences of the 1970s and 1980s played a pivotal role in reshaping global attitudes toward CBI. The Federal Reserve, the Deutsche Bundesbank, and the Swiss National Bank emerged as exemplars. The Volcker/Bundesbank approach, advocating an independent central bank with a mandate to curb inflation, gained traction globally.

The Treaty of Maastricht in 1992 made CBI a prerequisite for European Currency Union membership, and establishing the European Central Bank in 1999 marked the pinnacle of central bank independence. Despite occasional concerns about the "democracy deficit," the ECB's independence has remained unthreatened. In responding to the mega-crises of 2007-9 and 2020-21, the Fed collaborated closely with the Treasury, prompting debates about potential subordination of the central bank. While critics viewed this collaboration as compromising Fed independence, the Fed successfully defended its powers during the Dodd-Frank Act discussions in 2010. The more recent episode during the COVID-19 crisis saw the Fed engaged in unconventional measures, cooperating extensively with the Treasury. The Fed's involvement in unique lending facilities, such as the Main Street Lending Program, stirred debates about the boundaries of its traditional roles. The question of who was subordinated to whom remains open, raising crucial considerations for the future.

Chair Jerome Powell consistently emphasized that the Federal Reserve's primary role is to engage in lending rather than spending, indicating an expectation of avoiding losses on its loans. To reconcile this stance, Congress navigated a solution by assigning the Small Business Administration the responsibility of absorbing any losses incurred from Paycheck Protection Program loans. Although these loans, destined never to be repaid, represented an unconventional addition to the Fed's balance sheet, the central bank supported assuming these new duties during the unique and urgent circumstances of 2020. Despite these unprecedented developments, the Fed's acquiescence to these responsibilities during the exceptional conditions of 2020 suggests that central bank independence is poised to endure the post-COVID-19 era as long as the ensuing economic landscape aligns with the established norms.

Policy Challenges for the Next 50 Years

The world economy remains fragile after more than five years since the global financial and economic crisis, with growth in key regions still below pre-crisis levels. Unemployment rates in the OECD are persistently high, and productive capacity has deteriorated. To bolster recovery and minimize the risks of relapsing into stagnation, monetary policy must remain highly accommodative, while fiscal consolidation should align with existing plans. Additionally, there is a crucial need for growth-promoting structural reforms in both OECD countries and many emerging economies, coupled with enhancing stability in the financial sector. Implementing such comprehensive policies can contribute to a robust recovery, preventing long-term damage to potential growth resulting from the crisis and gradually eliminating economic slack. Looking ahead to the next 50 years, a significant shift in economic balance is anticipated, particularly towards emerging economies in Asia. By 2060, the share of non-OECD countries in global GDP is expected to surpass that of the current OECD area. Economic growth, especially in Asia, will continue to lift millions out of poverty and integrate them into the global economy.

Despite this, the global growth outlook until 2060 appears modest compared to the past. GDP in the OECD and emerging G20 countries is projected to grow 2.7 percent from 2010 to 2060, compared to 3.4 percent from 1996 to 2010. Global GDP is forecasted to expand by 3.0 percent annually from 2010 to 2060, resulting in a 350 percent increase. While emerging economies will experience more sustained growth than the OECD, it will decelerate due to the gradual exhaustion of the catch-up process and less favorable demographics across most countries. Population aging will lead to a decline in the potential labor force, only partially offset by increases in labor force participation and employment rates. Future GDP per capita gains will increasingly hinge on skill accumulation, innovation, and knowledge-based capital. In particular, Asian growth could face further constraints due to escalating economic damages from environmental degradation, primarily driven by climate change, which may impact these countries earlier than anticipated. By 2060, environmental damages in South and Southeast Asia could reduce GDP by over 5 percent compared to the central scenario.

Global integration is expected to persist but at a slower pace. Trade intensity is likely to increase significantly, and by 2060, euro area exports to Asia and emerging economies might reach 15 percent of GDP, comparable in size to trade within the eurozone. While increased cross-country interdependence can help share the burdens of shocks globally, it also makes the global economy more susceptible to imbalances. It needs to improve the effectiveness of various domestic policy instruments. As the skill composition, capital intensity, and consumption patterns of emerging economies converge towards those of the OECD, their production structures will increasingly resemble those in OECD countries.

Addressing the Challenge of Sluggish Growth

Policymakers must enact strategic changes to address the underlying causes of sluggish growth. Countries can enhance growth prospects by focusing on four pivotal areas: expediting global integration (including promoting migration flows), fortifying institutions against shocks (e.g., demographic shifts), mitigating climate change by reducing emissions and harnessing the potential of the knowledge economy—the primary driver of future global growth. The following policy recommendations would help enhance growth:

1. Multilateral Trade and Investment Agreements:

- Implement additional agreements to boost trade and investment.

- Pursue migration policies targeting skill and labor gaps.
- Support entrepreneurial activity and worker mobility through policies like pension portability.

2. Social Insurance Reforms:

- Reform social insurance to sustain the workforce in the face of longevity and aging challenges.
- Strengthen retirement systems against productivity and demographic shocks.

3. Education and Skills Development:

- Translate the strong demand for education and skills into job-relevant skills.
- Address the demand for jobs by ensuring product and labor market settings facilitate the expansion of young and high-productive firms.

3. Environmental Sustainability:

- Take early action to prevent environmental damage from impeding growth.
- Shift towards a cleaner development path through carbon pricing, fossil-fuel subsidy reforms, and targeted measures.

While pro-growth policies may involve trade-offs, careful considerations are essential. For instance, financing increased investment in tertiary education with public funds could raise public spending in OECD countries by an average of 1 percent of GDP by 2060. To address this, reforms should ensure that beneficiaries of higher education bear a larger share of the funding burden.

Deep-seated trade-offs may arise as knowledge and skills become the primary drivers of growth, potentially leading to increased tensions and inequalities. Without intervention, these inequalities could reach comparable levels in the United States today. Managing structural adjustments will be crucial to workers' well-being, especially in emerging economies. However, addressing these tensions and inequalities through domestic public policy may face limitations, such as fiscal constraints and increased cross-country mobility of tax bases. Addressing this conundrum requires a diverse set of policy tools:

1. Equality of Opportunities in Education: Focus public resources on early years and lifelong learning initiatives.
2. Tax and Welfare System Adjustments: Adapt tax and welfare systems to increase the mobility of capital and labor.
3. Shift taxation towards immovable factors and reform employment regulations to support workers' mobility.
4. Broadening Welfare Systems: Expand welfare systems to provide insurance against shocks and macroeconomic risks and ensure conditionality for sustainability.
5. Global Coordination and Cooperation: Cooperate globally for trade and investment liberalization.
6. Coordinate tax bases and environmental policies due to their cross-border impacts.
7. Address challenges related to knowledge-based capital through international cooperation.

As the world becomes more multipolar, policymakers must navigate complex coordination challenges with emerging economies, necessitating global collaboration in climate change mitigation, intellectual property rights, and competition law enforcement.

Review Questions

1. How has fiscal policy evolved, incorporating insights from different economic schools?
2. What are the key constraints on the effectiveness of fiscal policy, and how do high public debt levels impact its implementation?
3. Discuss the ideological shifts in economic policy, particularly the challenges faced by Keynesianism in the late 1960s.
4. How did the global financial crisis impact the adoption of Keynesian policies, and what were the subsequent shifts in political attitudes towards fiscal measures?
5. Explain the evolving patterns of fiscal policy under different U.S. presidents, considering their stated ideologies and actual policy actions.
6. What role has Central Bank Independence (CBI) played in shaping monetary-fiscal dynamics, and how has it evolved over the years?

Discussion Points

1. Evaluate the effectiveness of fiscal policy during major economic crises, considering the pragmatic shifts observed in policy responses.
2. Discuss the challenges political ideologies face in implementing consistent fiscal policies and the implications for economic stability.
3. Explore the implications of the evolving landscape of fiscal policy and Central Bank Independence for future economic management, particularly in the face of potential global challenges.

CHAPTER FOUR: FISCAL POLICY OF THE FUTURE: ADAPTING NATIONAL POLICIES TO GLOBAL TRANSFORMATIONS

1. Changing Landscape of National Policymaking:

   - Economic growth is expected to decelerate, with innovation and knowledge-based assets becoming crucial.
   - Uneven distribution of benefits may intensify the trade-off between growth and equity.
   - Global integration and competition for knowledge-based activities pose challenges to traditional redistributive tools.

2. Promoting Equity Amid Challenges:

   - Deliberate policies are needed to promote equity, especially in education and training.
   - Fiscal pressures and eroding tax bases present risks to equity promotion.
   - Increased economic interdependence necessitates enhanced international policy coordination.

3. Global Economic Shifts (2020-2060):

   - Pivot toward emerging economies, particularly in Asia.
   - Anticipated slowdown in global GDP growth, influenced by factors like

MFP slowdown and demographic changes.
- Growing trade integration, but earning inequalities and income dispersion are expected to persist and intensify.

4. Public Spending Impact in Low-Income Countries:

- Effective allocation of expenditures is crucial for low-income countries benefiting from debt relief.
- The correlation between public spending levels and outcomes is inconclusive; inefficiencies and inequities may diminish the positive impact.
- Specific increases in education and health spending are linked to positive outcomes.

5. Taxation Strategies for Development:

- Developing nations need help in establishing efficient tax systems.
- Corporate tax revenues are declining, necessitating alternative revenue sources.
- The distributional effects of tax reforms on income inequality must be considered for development goals.

6. Foreign Aid and Macroeconomic Challenges:

- Concessional loans are associated with higher domestic revenue mobilization; grants may not increase aggregate resources in corrupt countries.
- Aid allocation criteria present dilemmas, and aid volatility challenges fiscal policy management.
- Flexibility in fiscal frameworks proposed to navigate challenges associated with aid volatility.

Changing Landscape of National Policy Making: Challenges and Shifts

Over the next few decades, the conditions for national policymaking are poised for substantial change. Economic growth is anticipated to decelerate, especially in the advanced economies, with innovation and knowledge-based assets emerging as pivotal drivers. However, the benefits of this evolution are expected to be unevenly distributed among income groups and countries, intensifying the trade-off between growth and equity. As global integration advances and international competition for knowledge-based activities heightens, conventional redistributive tools like taxes and transfers may face greater challenges within countries.

The Need to Deliberately Promote Equity: To address this dynamic, policies promoting equity in opportunity, particularly in education and training, could alleviate the growth-equity trade-off. However, these efforts must navigate mounting fiscal pressures and risks of eroding tax bases. As economic interdependence across borders intensifies, the repercussions of economic shocks are likely to be more widely shared among trading partners, diminishing volatility and risks for individual nations. Simultaneously, international spillover effects from policies may also increase, advocating for enhanced international policy coordination. Environmental concerns, especially related to climate change, are expected to escalate, acting as a drag on economic growth. Given the global nature of greenhouse gas emissions, effective mitigation necessitates coordinated global action.

Evolving Workable Strategies to Manage Global Challenges: While the demand for international policy coordination grows, policymakers must grapple with the world economy's increasing multipolarity, where emerging economies play a larger role. This complexity may hinder coordination efforts, exacerbated by the urgent yet challenging legacy of the recent crisis. Successfully managing global phenomena with significant spillovers, such as current account imbalances, migration flows, emissions, and intellectual property rights, requires overcoming these tensions.

Forecasts of Key Developments Over the Period 2020 - 2060

The world economy will pivot toward emerging economies, particularly in Asia. By 2060, non-OECD economies' share of global GDP will significantly surpass that of the current OECD area.

Global GDP Growth

Projected global GDP growth is expected to slow from 3.6 percent (2014–2030) to 2.7 percent (2030-2060). The key assumptions are reduced potential for catching up, slower increases in human capital stocks, and shrinking labor forces. Looking ahead to 2060, the potential growth trajectory in both OECD and non-OECD economies is anticipated to decelerate. While the increasing presence of fast-growing non-OECD economies in the global output is expected to mitigate the slowdown at the global level, several factors contribute to the moderation in growth among OECD and G20 countries.

Multifactor Productivity (MFP) slowdown is imminent: MFP growth is projected to decelerate across economies, aligning with a decrease in research and development (R&D) intensity growth. Average annual MFP growth in the OECD is forecasted to decline from 1.1 percent (decade to 2030) to 0.9 percent (to 2050). Rapidly growing non-OECD countries may experience a sharper slowdown in MFP growth as they converge toward OECD levels.

Slowing Pace of Educational Attainment: Although educational attainment levels will continue to rise, the pace of growth is expected to slow. The expected deceleration aligns with a scenario of roughly constant returns to investment in education.

Demographic Changes: The demographic dividend, stemming from rising participation rates and a lower share of dependent children and elderly citizens, will gradually diminish. The working-age population is anticipated to decline in certain regions, impacting labor's contribution to growth. Assumed retirement and labor market reforms aim to extend working lives in line with increasing longevity.

Global Trade Integration

Global trade integration will persist, albeit at a slightly slower pace. Exports from non-OECD countries are set to rise from 35 percent (2012) to 56 percent (2060) of world exports. The underlying assumption is that more emerging economies will sprout from Africa, Latin America, South Asia, and former Soviet countries.

Global trade integration is predicted to deepen over the next 50 years, driven by falling transport costs and lowered trade barriers. The pace of integration, while ongoing, may slow without additional agreements to reduce barriers and transaction costs. Firms' strategies, technology advancements (e.g., 3D printing), and regional variations will influence evolving trade patterns.

However, despite growing trade integration, earning inequalities and income dispersion will persist and intensify, reflecting skill-biased technological change (SBTC) and a slower growth in educational attainment. Top gross earnings have outpaced lower-tier earnings, primarily due to the effects of SBTC. Predicting the future pace of SBTC is challenging, but assuming historical trends persist, earning dispersion may accelerate, growing between 17% and 40% within the OECD.

Income Inequality Factors: Rising capital incomes, less redistributive tax and benefit systems, and changing household formations increase income inequality. The widening gap in earnings, influenced by SBTC, has been a major driver of income dispersion. Assuming past trends continue, earning inequality could intensify, potentially affecting household disposable incomes.

It is crucial to note that while gross earning inequalities are expected to rise, real earnings are anticipated to grow across the spectrum. Nevertheless, the potential challenges of increasing earning inequality underscore the importance of effective redistributive policies. The following section will explore the consequences of policymaking in more detail.

Greenhouse Gas Emissions: Greenhouse gas emissions are predicted to double between 2010 and 2060. Potential economic impact includes a 1.5 percent reduction in global GDP in 2060 compared to the central scenario.

Despite advances in green energy development, fossil fuels will continue to drive development.

Earning Inequalities: Earning inequalities may rise by over 30 percent in the OECD area and around 20 percent in other G20 economies by 2060. The average OECD country could face inequality similar to the current U.S. experience, applying to today's less developed countries and regions.

Fiscal Challenges: Fiscal requirements to stabilize debt ratios may exceed 7 percent of GDP for the average OECD country by 2060. Additional fiscal risks include weakened revenues from reduced migration and more mobile tax bases.

Various models describing macroeconomics, trade, greenhouse gas emissions, and income inequality developments were employed to construct this central scenario. These interconnected models create a comprehensive framework for understanding the evolving global landscape. Long-term growth projections form the foundation, with subsequent modules providing insights into trade patterns, emissions, and inequality. The scenario envisions a shifting global economic order, demanding adept policy responses to navigate the challenges of a dynamically changing world.

Public Spending Impact in Low-Income Countries

Effective allocation of expenditures is paramount for low-income countries benefitting from debt relief. Many nations outline their poverty reduction plans through Poverty Reduction Strategy Papers (PRSPs), utilizing the additional resources from debt relief and donor contributions for poverty-alleviating programs. The ultimate goal is an enhanced performance in social indicators over time. However, a crucial question arises regarding the impact of higher public spending on desired outcomes. Existing evidence suggests that budgeted resources may only sometimes be utilized as intended.

Moreover, empirical findings on the correlation between public spending levels and outcomes, such as educational attainment and health status, are inconclusive. This lack of clear relationship can be attributed to various factors, including the potential crowding out of private spending on education and healthcare by public expenditure. Inefficiencies and inequities in the utilization of public resources may also diminish their positive impact on the well-being of people with low incomes. Gupta, Verhoeven, and Tiongson argue that specific increases in education and health spending positively influence related outcomes.

An increase in overall education spending, particularly on primary and secondary education as a share of total education spending, positively impacts educational attainment. Similarly, heightened healthcare spending is linked to reduced child and infant mortality rates. For instance, a one percentage point increase in education spending as a share of GDP may enhance gross secondary enrollment by over three percentage points. A 5-percentage point increase in the share of outlays for primary and secondary education in total education spending may lead to a more than one percentage point increase in gross secondary enrollment. Moreover, a one percentage point increase in health spending relative to GDP correlates with a decrease in infant and child mortality rates by about three deaths per 1,000 live births.

These findings emphasize the importance of focusing on the overall level of social spending and the allocation of resources within sectors. Despite limitations in data availability on indicator distribution among income classes, studies suggest that returns to public spending on health are notably higher among people experiencing poverty. Therefore, governments aiming to strengthen the connection between spending and outcomes for low-income people should prioritize improving the incidence and targeting of public spending.

Enhancing Education Access and Government Spending Efficiency

Ideally, all children should have access to high-quality, publicly funded education without financial barriers. Unfortunately, challenges arise when government resources are insufficient to provide free education or available funds are not directed toward their intended purposes. Cultural factors and user charges may also hinder children's access to education, leading to proposals that advocate against or seek the abolition of user payments for basic education. For example, a study by Hillman and Jenkner found instances where voluntary user payments played a crucial role, as parents took responsibility for their children's education in situations where access to schooling would otherwise be limited. This phenomenon can be attributed to the need for alternative financing or broader issues in public expenditure management. However, compulsory user payments might indicate administrative and governance obstacles in transitioning from regressive taxation to more broadly based taxation or could stem from inadequate donor funding for school financing.

In evaluating government spending efficiency on education and health across 37 African countries, Gupta and Verhoeven compare these regions with countries in Asia and the Western Hemisphere. The findings highlight substantial variations in how government spending influences measurable output indicators. On average, African governments demonstrate lower efficiency in providing health and education services than their Asian counterparts, with Asian governments appearing to be the most efficient. The results suggest that inefficiencies in African countries are not necessarily linked to private spending levels but may be attributed to relatively high government wages (in the case of education spending) and intra-sectoral allocation issues within the social sectors. The analysis proposes addressing these inefficiencies can improve educational attainment and health output indicators in Africa and the Western Hemisphere. Key areas for improvement include increasing allocations for primary education, optimizing allocations for curative health care, and ensuring that spending is effectively targeted to benefit lower-income groups, thus addressing expenditure inefficiencies.

Taxation Strategies for Development in Developing Countries

Developing nations grapple with substantial challenges in establishing efficient tax systems, primarily due to factors such as:

1. The prevalence of large informal sectors,
2. Inadequate availability of reliable data for effective monitoring and analysis,
3. Ineffective tax administrations, and

Influential high-income groups are hindering the introduction of more equitable taxes.

Addressing these challenges is crucial for enhancing revenue generation and facilitating development. Despite the complexity of the development process, a central question emerges: How can tax structures be improved within existing constraints? According to Keen and Simone, revenue in the poorest countries and regions of the developing world has, at best, remained stagnant; when seignorage is considered, it has generally decreased. While sales tax revenues have risen significantly due to the widespread implementation of the Value-Added Tax (VAT), efficiency gains from the VAT are not easily demonstrable. Future efforts should ensure the proper functioning of refund and credit mechanisms, integral to broader tax business reform. Additionally, trade tax revenues have substantially declined, posing challenges, especially for the poorest countries, in managing the revenue consequences of trade liberalization, which underscores the importance of sequencing trade reform and strengthening the domestic tax system.

The decline in corporate tax revenues in developing countries, as documented by Keen and Simone, is another concern. Unlike developed countries engaged in rate-reducing and base-broadening corporate tax reforms, developing countries have experienced rate reduction coupled with base reduction, partly due to international tax competition. Given that developing countries traditionally rely more on corporate tax revenues, this erosion may necessitate finding alternative revenue sources. Beyond revenue implications, tax policy also significantly influences income distribution. Evaluating the distributional effects of reform programs in low-income countries is increasingly recognized as essential. For instance, Muñoz and Cho analyze the distributive impact of introducing the VAT in Ethiopia, comparing it to the sales tax it replaced. Their findings reveal that the VAT is progressive but less so than the sales tax, hurting the poorest 40 per cent of the population. However, reallocating additional VAT revenues to primary education and health spending could make the poorest 40 per cent net beneficiaries. To meet development goals, developing countries must enhance the structure of their taxation systems and increase the overall revenues derived from these systems.

Foreign Aid: Loans vs. Grants and Macroeconomic Challenges

The effectiveness of foreign aid has long been debated, particularly concerning the efficiency of loans versus grants. Since the 1960s, a prevailing perspective has favored loans for their expected repayment, contrasting with recent calls for a shift towards grants to address issues of massive debt accumulation and the failure to achieve intended human development goals. Gupta, Clements, Pivorarsky, and Tiongson conducted an empirical analysis, revealing that concessional loans are associated with higher domestic revenue mobilization, while grants have the opposite effect. In highly corrupt countries, grants may not increase the aggregate resources available for government expenditure, unlike loans that avoid this drawback.

Examining macroeconomic challenges, Heller and Gupta contemplate the implications of industrial countries meeting the international target of allocating 0.7 percent of GNP, about $175 billion, in development assistance. The criteria for aid allocation across countries present a dilemma, with considerations for massive transfers to the least developed countries potentially overwhelming their economies. If distributed proportionally to the share of the world's absolute poor, aid may disproportionately benefit larger countries. Capacity issues in absorbing these funds, macroeconomic challenges, and potential aid dependence need addressing for any significant expansion of Official Development Assistance (ODA).

Lane and Bulíř examine the volatility and unpredictability of aid inflows, emphasizing their impact on fiscal policy management in aid-receiving countries. They find aid significantly more volatile than domestic fiscal revenue, exacerbating rather than smoothing cyclical shocks. Flexible fiscal frameworks, adjusted tax and spending plans, and built-in fiscal flexibility are proposed as strategies to navigate the challenges associated with aid volatility. The study underscores the need for a comprehensive effort by the development community to anticipate and address challenges in utilizing external resources effectively.

Food Aid: Implications for Stability and Fiscal Management

The findings of Lane and Bulíř on aid procyclicality are significant, highlighting that aid flows generally cannot effectively stabilize consumption fluctuations. This observation prompts an exploration of various aid forms, including Official Development Assistance (ODA), technical assistance, and food aid. Gupta, Clements, and Tiongson specifically examine the role of food aid, aiming to assess its effectiveness in stabilizing food consumption in recipient countries and its targeted distribution to the most vulnerable nations. Their investigation concludes that food aid is acyclical, indicating neither a pro- nor countercyclical nature, which has profound implications for macroeconomic and fiscal management. Firstly, if food aid is not distributed countercyclically and recipient governments depend on counterpart funds generated from the sale of aid-provided commodities as a revenue source, the instability of budgetary revenues persists during declines in food production and output. Secondly, shortages in food supply place additional burdens on government budgets to implement programs shielding the population's consumption. Without counterpart funds from food aid, governments must tap into domestic resources to fund such programs. Consequently, falling revenues and heightened demand for budgetary programs can complicate macroeconomic management for countries receiving food aid. In such scenarios, food aid fails to function as an "automatic stabilizer."

Public Finance, Armed Conflict, Terrorism, and Development: A Macro-Fiscal Perspective

Countries emerging from conflict, such as Iraq, Afghanistan, and the Democratic Republic of Congo, confront distinct challenges in devising and executing effective macroeconomic and fiscal policies. Establishing an institutional framework grounded in a straightforward yet realistic policy stance is crucial for restoring macroeconomic stability and setting the groundwork for renewed growth. These nations typically grapple with a collapsed revenue base and extraordinary expenditure needs in the fiscal realm. While numerous studies have explored the economic ramifications of armed conflict and terrorism, few have delved into their fiscal implications.

Various studies have scrutinized the economic costs of armed conflicts, revealing an inverse relationship between measures of political instability, violence, and indicators of growth and investment. For instance, Arunatilake, Jayasuriya, and Kelegama (2001) estimate that Sri Lanka incurred costs approximately twice its 1996 GDP during the conflict from 1983 to 1996. Prolonged terrorist activities, akin to armed conflicts, have been shown to directly and indirectly impede growth. Walkenhorst and Dihel (2002) estimate global welfare losses of about $75 billion due to heightened security measures after the September 11, 2001 attacks. Gupta, Clements, Bhattacharya, and Chakravarti find that countries successfully resolving conflicts and addressing terrorism experience substantial economic gains, encompassing enhanced economic growth, macroeconomic stability, and increased tax revenues to support poverty-alleviating expenditures. Furthermore, the results suggest that nations affected by conflict and terrorism are likely to witness a rebound in government tax revenues and a decline in military spending (albeit with a lag) after violence ceases, contributing to restoring macroeconomic stability. These findings underscore the potential of a "peace dividend" to foster economic development.

Strengthening Fiscal Policy through Institutional Reform in Africa

The effectiveness of fiscal policy hinges on robust institutional frameworks, particularly in expenditure management. The efficiency of additional aid flows in addressing poverty reduction and improving social indicators is contingent on well-functioning expenditure management systems. Lienert's analysis delves into the disparities between the public expenditure management systems of Anglophone and Francophone Africa. Contrary to expectations, although Francophone countries possess potentially advantageous budget execution and government accounting systems, they have yet to translate into superior results.

The suboptimal performance is attributed not to the inherent deficiencies of the public expenditure management systems in Anglophone and Francophone countries but to operational shortcomings. Even with clarified budget legislation and implementation instructions, significant improvements are only possible with a simultaneous shift in the behavior of key stakeholders across the executive, legislative, and judicial branches of government. Enhancing budget discipline and ensuring accountability throughout the budget process—preparation, execution, and reporting—emerges as a critical imperative. Lasting improvements demand stringent enforcement of existing rules, accompanied by sanctions where necessary. Achieving this necessitates strong political will in both Anglophone and Francophone Africa. While primarily a domestic concern, the international community can contribute by gaining a more comprehensive understanding of how public expenditure management systems operate and conditioning foreign assistance on demonstrated efforts to enhance public sector accountability.

Review Questions

1. How does the evolving global economic order influence the trade-off between growth and equity in national policymaking?
2. What are the key assumptions and factors contributing to the anticipated

slowdown in global GDP growth from 2014 to 2060?

3. Discuss the challenges low-income countries face in effectively utilizing debt relief for poverty-alleviating programs.

4. How do taxation structures impact income distribution in developing countries, and what challenges do they face in improving tax systems?

5. Evaluate the effectiveness of concessional loans versus grants in the context of foreign aid, considering domestic revenue mobilization and corruption.

6. What strategies are proposed to address the challenges associated with aid volatility and its impact on fiscal policy management?

Discussion Points

1. Explore the implications of the shift toward emerging economies, particularly in Asia, on global economic dynamics and national policymaking.

2. Discuss the role of international policy coordination in addressing economic interdependence and global integration challenges.

3. Examine the potential trade-offs and synergies between promoting economic growth and ensuring equity in the context of evolving global challenges.

CHAPTER FIVE: GROWTH IMPERATIVES FOR 2060: PRIORITIZING FISCAL REFORMS FOR KNOWLEDGE-BASED GROWTH

Summary of Key Points

1. Post-COVID-19 Fiscal Reform Challenges:

- Global fiscal challenges post-COVID-19 demand substantial efforts across countries.
- Fiscal pressures arise from demographic shifts, escalating spending, and health and education demands.
- Fiscal consolidation through reforms, including pension reforms, is envisioned for 2030 and beyond.

2. Global Imbalances and Fiscal Pressures:

- Several countries face significant fiscal consolidation tasks, especially in Europe and Japan.
- Adverse shifts in real interest rates and demographic changes intensify fiscal challenges.
- Fiscal consolidation and structural reforms are crucial for mitigating

medium-term global imbalances.

3. Uncertain Future Productivity and Education Dynamics:

- Future multifactor productivity (MFP) growth is uncertain, driven by knowledge-based capital and reforms.
- The debate on the impact of ICT on productivity has intensified amid recent slowdowns.
- Challenges in tertiary education and demand for skilled workers pose complexities for future growth.

4. MIRAGE-e Model and Potential Risks:

- The MIRAGE-e model identifies risks like trade-driven productivity growth, demographic shifts, and emissions.
- Economic migration, greenhouse gas emissions, and fiscal pressures are pivotal considerations.
- Emerging economies share comparable fiscal challenges, emphasizing the interconnectedness of global factors.

5. Economic Impacts of Climate Change:

- Climate change poses significant threats, impacting biodiversity, water scarcity, and premature deaths.
- Greenhouse gas emissions are a major global risk with potential long-term economic damages.
- Impacts on GDP by 2060 vary across regions, with agriculture and rising sea levels being critical factors.

6. Policy Recommendations for Growth:

- Key policy areas include trade liberalization, international R&D collaboration, and intellectual property rights.

- Enabling factors like private R&D, competition policies, and structural change policies are vital.
- Policy considerations include adapting to demographic shifts, flexible labor markets, and meeting education demand.

Post-COVID-19 Fiscal Reform Challenges and Global Imbalance Considerations

Addressing fiscal challenges on a global scale demands substantial efforts across various countries. The aftermath of the COVID-19 crisis, unfavorable demographic shifts, and escalating spending pressures in critical areas such as health and education create significant fiscal pressures. In the central scenario, a resolution to these pressures is envisioned through fiscal and structural reforms. Medium-term fiscal consolidation, targeted for 2030, augments revenues and curbs expenditures. Post-2030, pension reforms are expected to maintain pension spending relative to GDP, while other spending areas are assumed to remain constant. Despite these relatively optimistic assumptions, several countries face a noteworthy fiscal consolidation task, albeit smaller than the efforts made by some European crisis-stricken nations. Estimations of the required fiscal consolidation to reach the 60 percent public debt threshold by 2060, based on initial fiscal gaps and assumed constant spending ratios, indicate substantial efforts. The UK and Spain face gaps exceeding 5 percent of GDP, while Japan's gap exceeds 13 percent. The challenge intensifies if anticipated increases in pension, health, and education spending ratios are factored in.

For heavily indebted nations, the scenario could worsen due to adverse shifts in real interest rates. Demographic changes affecting savings may elevate real interest rates by up to three-quarters of a point between 2015 and 2060, impacting public finances, particularly in high-debt scenarios. Additional pressures may arise from replacing aging infrastructure, transitioning to a greener economy, or addressing climate change effects. Fiscal consolidation and structural reforms are imperative to mitigate medium-term global imbalances. While global current account imbalances diminished during the crisis, they persist at elevated levels compared to the pre-2000 period. Long-term demographic trends and accelerated aging in surplus countries might contribute to lower imbalances. Rising interest rates in net debtor nations could also suppress investment, influencing imbalances. However, sustained reduction requires further policy intervention. Ambitious fiscal consolidation, particularly in the United States, euro area deficit nations, and Japan, holds the potential to stabilize imbalances. The conjunction of fiscal consolidation with structural reforms could initiate a decline in imbalances.

Persistent increases in inequality may influence saving and investment dynamics, impacting global imbalances. The central scenario underscores that widespread and substantial inequality hikes may prompt heightened savings, with high-income households exhibiting higher savings rates. Countries witnessing rising inequality might witness improved current accounts if capital is fully mobile across borders. However, caution is warranted, as prolonged inequality growth could contribute to new financial imbalances. The argument linking rising inequality to falling real interest rates suggests a complex interplay of factors, including credit growth, financial intermediation, and leverage, which played a role in the recent financial crisis. Balancing these effects against factors such as decreasing global savings due to aging and lower precautionary savings in large emerging markets becomes essential.

The Uncertain Terrain of Future Productivity and Education Dynamics

The future trajectory of multifactor productivity (MFP) growth, a key contributor to GDP per capita, carries uncertainties. In the central scenario, MFP is expected to account for 75 percent of the growth in OECD and major non-member economies up to 2060. While the pace of MFP growth may ease over time, it is anticipated to remain comparatively high, propelled by substantial investments in knowledge-based capital (KBC) and pro-competition reforms. The uncertainty lies in the future growth rate of frontier ideas, with contrasting views shaping the discussion. Optimists envision a cascade of innovations driven by the full potential of information and communication technology (ICT), propelling the technological frontier forward. Pessimists, however, argue that the impact of the ICT revolution has waned, and future inventions may not significantly alter trend productivity. The ongoing debate is intensified by the recent productivity slowdown in many OECD countries, with challenges distinguishing between cyclical impacts and changes in frontier growth.

Regardless of the unfolding scenario, countries with a substantial stock of knowledge-based assets are better poised to adapt to changes in frontier growth. The accumulation of such assets can be fostered through effective government policies. The rise in trade integration is expected to accelerate international technology diffusion, further boosting MFP growth. This dynamic effect is vital for countries distant from the technology frontier, posing an upside risk to growth beyond the baseline projection.

In parallel, the growing demand for highly educated workers challenges tertiary education systems, impacting growth and equity. While educational attainment levels are projected to rise, the rate of increase is anticipated to slow, aligning with constant returns to investment in education. Earning inequalities may escalate due to the knowledge-oriented global economy, amplifying the need for education. OECD analysis suggests that if demand for tertiary education reacts as in the past, it could outpace the central scenario in most countries. The critical question arises: Can tertiary education supply expand to meet this heightened demand? If successful, it could boost skill development, foster growth, and mitigate increases in inequality compared to the central scenario. Conversely, failure to meet this demand could lead to lower growth and heightened inequalities. There will also be a growing demand for a highly skilled but less educated (low-certified) workforce.

MIRAGE-e Model - Identifying Potential Risks, Tensions, and Consequences

We employ the MIRAGE-e model that allows for regional and sectoral aggregation tailored to specific applications and highlights key assumptions related to product quality ranges, imperfect competition, Foreign Direct Investment (FDI), and dynamic aspects. MIRAGE, developed by CEPII in 2001, is a multi-sector, multi-country CGE model initially designed for trade policy analysis and later applied to long-term growth and environmental issues. Users of MIRAGE include CEPII and various institutions such as IFPRI, INRAE, ITC, UNECA, DG Enterprise, and DG Trade at the European Commission. On the demand side, final consumption is modeled through a representative agent in each region, employing a Cobb-Douglas function and Linear Expenditure System - Constant Elasticity of Substitution (LES-CES) function to account for changing demand structures. The nesting of CES functions considers factors like product differentiation based on geographical origin and horizontal differentiation between varieties. Total demand comprises final consumption, intermediate consumption, and capital goods. The regional representative agent includes the government, handling taxes implicitly through the representative agent's budget constraint. On the supply side, production utilizes five factors: capital, skilled labor, unskilled labor, land, and natural resources. Factor endowments are assumed to be fully employed, with exogenous growth rates for natural resources and labor. Land and capital allocation is endogenous, and the model considers the possibility of extending arable land. Labor mobility varies within agricultural and non-agricultural sectors within each country.

Trade-Driven Productivity Growth: The MIRAGE-e model suggests that heightened trade intensities may lead to faster productivity growth than anticipated. A prolonged information and communication technology (ICT) wave could further boost growth, while a slowdown in frontier productivity growth could have adverse effects.

Demographic Shifts and Economic Migration: Demographic projections might be overly optimistic, especially when considering factors influencing economic migration. Models predicting international migrant stocks indicate potential reversals or drying up migration flows into the OECD due to income convergence between host and home countries.

Greenhouse Gas Emissions and Economic Impact: Projections of greenhouse gas emissions and subsequent temperature increases could impact economic activity and specialization patterns. Models incorporating these environmental factors suggest that GDP might be lower in the long run than projected in the central scenario.

Tertiary Education Dynamics: Demand and supply for tertiary education may deviate from the central scenario due to changes in returns to education. Models indicate a potential rise in demand for tertiary graduations, driven by increasing GDP per capita and earning differentials, leading to higher growth and lower earning inequality if adequately funded.

Work-Related Migration and Economic Incentives: Income convergence between OECD countries and developing economies may diminish work-related migration flows, exacerbating labor shortages in the OECD, which could lead to unexpected net emigration of economic migrants from OECD countries, impacting the labor force and GDP.

Fiscal Pressures and Needed Reforms: The scale of required structural and fiscal reforms to stabilize public debt at 60 percent of GDP is substantial. Fiscal challenges, particularly in health, pension, and education spending, pose a significant downside risk to the fiscal position in the central scenario for OECD countries.

Similar Fiscal Challenges in Emerging Economies: Emerging economies face comparable fiscal challenges, with demographic pressures, rising health expenditures, and the need for expanded education systems. These challenges will likely be more pronounced in emerging economies than in the OECD.

The above scenarios highlight the complexity and interconnectedness of various factors, urging a comprehensive understanding and proactive consideration of potential risks and consequences in future planning.

Economic Impacts and Global Risks of Climate Change Pressures

Climate change will continue to exert significant strains on the environment, given the continued use of fossil fuels, hastened urbanization, and the attendant pressure on the environment. Projections indicate a concerning scenario by 2050: a further 10 percent decline in terrestrial biodiversity, 40 percent of the global population residing in high water scarcity regions, a doubling of premature deaths linked to airborne particulate matter, and an impending lock-in of disruptive climate change due to a substantial surge in greenhouse gas emissions. Among these trends, the escalating concentrations of greenhouse gases emerge as the most comprehensive global risk to economic well-being. In the absence of transformative shifts in the carbon intensity of global energy practices, continuous economic growth is poised to drive an incessant rise in greenhouse gas (GHG) emissions, contributing to an escalating concentration of these gases in the atmosphere, which not only heightens the threat of costly climatic shifts but also worsens other environmental challenges. The share of non-OECD countries in global economic output will surge, underscoring their increasing contributions to these emissions. Although the most substantial economic damages from unchecked GHG emissions are predicted to occur post-2060, rising global temperatures may affect GDP earlier.

Braconier and Dellink (2014) predicted a possible reduction in world GDP by 2060, ranging between 0.7 percent and 2.5 percent due to selected climate change impacts. Climate change's influence on economic performance manifests through various channels, with declining agricultural productivity and losses in capital and land from rising sea levels expected to be pivotal contributors to GDP impacts by 2060 on a global scale. The magnitude of this impact hinges on geographical, climatic conditions, and prevailing specialization patterns, leading to varied and region-specific climate change damages. Regions experiencing high-temperature variability, boasting signif-icant agricultural sectors, and facing vulnerability to rising sea levels might endure severe consequences, with potential damages in South and South-East Asia surpassing 5 percent of GDP by 2060. Conversely, more temperate regions could initially witness benefits outweighing losses, including higher agricultural productivity, improved trade terms, and, in some instances, heightened demand for tourist services. However, the sustainability of these benefits remains to be determined.

Key Policy Recommendations for Bolstering Growth

Trade Liberalization Agreements: Further agreements on trade liberalization, particularly on a global scale, have the potential to boost growth, especially in emerging economies significantly. Multilateral trade liberalization is more beneficial globally than regional agreements, with anticipated limited effects on wage differentials.

International Collaboration in Research and Development (R&D): Given the increasing global interconnectivity and the crucial role of Multinational Enterprises (MNEs) in global business R&D, mechanisms for funding and supporting basic research should be considered. Coordinated efforts in tax treatment of R&D incentives may also be necessary to align with this global shift.

Intellectual Property Rights (IPRs): While IPRs play a crucial role in investment in certain knowledge-based assets, international coordination and review of IPR approaches are recommended to balance fostering innovation and avoiding hindrances, especially in areas like Information and Communication Technology (ICT).

Enabling Factors

Private R&D and high-quality management enhance the capacity to effectively absorb and deploy new technologies, thereby supporting productivity growth.

Competition Policies: Fostering competition, both domestically and in international markets, through closer cooperation among competition authorities complements IPR efforts and stimulates the development of growth-enabling factors.

Adapting to Structural Change: Despite limited evidence of a rise in the pace of structural change in the next 50 years, attention should be directed towards an aging workforce. Policies should shift focus from search activities to work incentives and retraining to mitigate potential mismatches in the labor market.

Longevity Adjustment in Retirement Ages: As populations age, adjusting retirement ages becomes crucial to counteract negative labor supply and growth effects from aging demographics.

Flexible Labor Markets and Migration-Friendly Policies: A combination of labor and product market flexibility, along with migration-friendly policies, can enhance both migration and labor supply, contributing to economic growth.

Meeting Demand for Tertiary Education: Given widening earning differentials and longer working lives, there will be a rising demand for tertiary education. Supporting growth and equity entails making tuitions contribute a larger share of total costs and implementing lending schemes to address liquidity constraints and share rising earning risks.

Lifelong Learning Strategies: As working lives extend due to increased longevity, strategies and funding for lifelong learning need strengthening. Public funding for older workers may be wider than for younger tertiary students.

Economic Impact of Trade Liberalization: Balancing Growth and Challenges

Recent research by the OECD explores the potential consequences of further multilateral and regional trade liberalization. The multilateral scenario envisions a 50 percent reduction in tariffs on goods, a 25 percent decrease in transaction costs, significant cuts in regulatory barriers, and a 50 percent reduction in agricultural support in key economies. As a result of these liberalization efforts, world trade could surge by 15% by 2060, leading to shifts in specialization patterns, particularly toward increased service production in emerging economies. The economic benefits would vary, with some OECD economies gaining 0.5 percent of GDP and India potentially experiencing an 8 percent boost. However, implementing well-designed framework policies and institutions is crucial to facilitating trade, given international transactions' inherent costs and risks.

Framework Policies and Potential Side Effects: Navigating Trade-Offs

While reforms in framework policies are essential for maximizing trade benefits, they may also introduce challenges that warrant careful consideration and potential counteractive measures:

Financial Sector Implications: Access to financial services is pivotal for trade financing and managing exchange rate risks. A larger financial sector, measured by credit-to-GDP ratios, correlates with higher exports, especially in sectors reliant on external financing. Nevertheless, higher credit-to-GDP ratios pose financial risks that could impede economic growth.

Trade Liberalization and Inequality: While trade liberalization tends to boost GDP, it may also exacerbate domestic inequality. Empirical analyses suggest that rising trade exposure correlates with lower labor shares of GDP, indicating potential benefits skewed towards more mobile capital than less mobile labor. However, the impact of widening income differentials remains a matter of debate, and compensating mechanisms might play a role.

Social Costs and Structural Adjustment: Trade reforms trigger resource reallocation across sectors, occupations, and firms. While integrating certain countries into the global trade system may enhance aggregate welfare, individual sectors may experience significant income fluctuations. Dealing with relative wage pressures and the need for structural adjustments due to rising trade integration is crucial, although similar challenges arise from changing demand structures or technological shifts.

Supporting Knowledge-Based Growth: Policy Considerations

Future growth will hinge increasingly on rising multifactor productivity expected to contribute 54 percent to 88 percent of GDP per capita in OECD countries from 2010 to 2060. In non-OECD G20 countries, this contribution may rise from 79 percent to almost 91 percent. Policies targeting Knowledge-Based Capital (KBC) will become pivotal, falling into two categories: those supporting knowledge creation, technology development, and absorption, and those influencing the effective utilization of new technologies. The globalization of innovation is evident in the rapid scientific advancements in emerging economies and the outsourcing of Research and Development (R&D). The growth of knowledge-based assets hinges on the accumulation of mobile resources like skilled labor and Foreign Direct Investment (FDI). Therefore, countries' ability to meet projected growth rates may rely on their capacity to attract such resources. This could lead to policy competition among nations, such as alterations in personal income and corporate tax policies to entice investments and managerial talent. To mitigate potential harm to growth, cross-country tax policy coordination may offer benefits, preventing fiscal pressures or excessive reallocation of factors.

Global Innovation from Cross-Country Collaboration: The increasingly global nature of innovation calls for enhanced cross-country coordination in specific areas. Publicly funded research, a catalyst for new general-purpose technologies, demands sustained funding to propel future growth, especially for transitioning to a greener economy reliant on novel technologies. The benefits of such research are expanding globally due to intensified international trade integration and improved communication technologies, generating larger positive spillovers. However, this global diffusion of knowledge may present challenges for countries seeking to appropriate the benefits, necessitating potential international coordination in funding basic research.

Increase Deployment of Cross-Border Tax Strategies: As global integration intensifies, multinational enterprises may employ cross-border tax strategies to shift profits from Knowledge-Based Capital (KBC) across countries. This could inadvertently result in high total tax support for R&D, placing domestic firms solely engaged in R&D at a competitive disadvantage. International co-operation is seen as valuable in limiting unintended tax relief for R&D arising from cross-border tax planning. The OECD underscores the advantages of designing R&D support schemes that do not favor incumbents over innovative young firms.

Convergence in per capita income between the OECD and emerging economies, coupled with evolving international specialization patterns, is blurring the distinction between innovating advanced economy firms and imitating emerging economy firms. This trend prompts the need for increased international policy coordination on Intellectual Property Rights (IPR) protection. The dynamic nature of technological change requires frequent updates to IPR regimes. In sectors with fragmented innovation processes, like software, existing patent systems may disproportionately favor incumbents, posing a policy dilemma that necessitates attention. In addition to revisiting IPR regimes, pro-competitive reforms in domestic product market regulations could serve as another avenue to overcome barriers to KBC accumulation created by existing patent systems. IPR regimes are most effective when coupled with pro-competition policies. With ongoing globalization, promoting the accumulation of knowledge-based assets through competition will likely require greater cross-border cooperation between competition authorities. While global cooperation has improved, future efforts may involve pursuing multilateral agreements and developing international standards to enhance collaboration among competition authorities, extending beyond mere information sharing to formalized cooperation in enforcement.

Review Questions

1. What are the key challenges in post-COVID-19 fiscal reforms, and how are they interconnected globally?
2. Explain the role of fiscal consolidation and structural reforms in address-

ing medium-term global imbalances.

3. What uncertainties surround future multifactor productivity (MFP) growth, and how do knowledge-based assets contribute to it?

4. How does the MIRAGE-e model identify potential risks, and what are the considerations for emerging economies?

5. Discuss the economic impacts of climate change, focusing on the inter-connectedness with greenhouse gas emissions.

6. Evaluate the policy recommendations for growth, emphasizing the role of trade liberalization and knowledge-based capital.

Discussion Points

1. Interconnected Global Challenges:

- Explore the interconnected nature of fiscal challenges, demographic shifts, and global imbalances.
- Discuss the potential spillover effects of fiscal reforms in one country on the global economic landscape.

2. Trade Liberalization and Inequality:

- Debate the potential trade-off between the economic benefits of trade liberalization and its impact on domestic inequality.
- Discuss strategies to mitigate the adverse effects of trade liberalization on income distribution.

3. Global Cooperation in Climate Change Mitigation:

- Discuss the need for enhanced international cooperation in addressing climate change and its economic consequences.
- Explore potential mechanisms for collaboration among nations to achieve sustainable environmental practices.

CHAPTER SIX: STRATEGIC STRUCTURAL REFORMS FOR SUSTAINABLE GROWTH AND EQUITY

Summary of Key Points

1. Role of National Policies in Technological Advancement:

- Effective national policies emphasizing Knowledge-Based Capital (KBC) accumulation, competition, and innovation maximize benefits from technological change.
- Information and Communication Technology (ICT) integration within organizational changes is crucial for technology leverage.
- Enabling factors like managerial quality and private sector R&D are vital for adapting to technological frontiers.
- Government policies, reducing Product Market Regulations (PMR), and promoting strong management practices impact a country's ability to benefit from technological growth.

2. Adapting Labor and Education Policies to Changing Demographics:

- Adjusting retirement age and implementing immigration-friendly policies are necessary responses to unfavorable demographics.
- Retirement reforms in two phases, potentially raising the retirement age

to 70-75, aim to maintain active labor participation.
- Proactive communication and strategic sequencing are essential for overcoming political obstacles in implementing necessary reforms.
- Well-designed immigration policies, including skills-based systems, can address labor shortages and attract diverse migrant groups.

3. Addressing Labor Market Dynamics in Evolving Demand:

- Adapting active labor market policies for different age groups is crucial in evolving labor demand structures.
- Extended working careers require a focus on on-the-job training and out-of-job retraining to address skill demands.
- Enhancing labor-market matching involves lowering employment protection to encourage hiring workers with evolving skills.
- Structural changes within sectors, driven by knowledge-based growth, necessitate nuanced policy responses.

4. Shaping Education Policies in Response to Skill Demands:

- Quality primary and secondary education is pivotal for increased participation in higher education and improved productivity.
- Adapting to longer working lives necessitates a stronger emphasis on life-long learning, particularly for older workers.
- Financial considerations, including potential co-payments for higher education, are crucial for addressing fiscal constraints.
- The evolution of education production, including online courses, challenges traditional education methods.

5. Switching to Loan Funding Models for Tertiary Education:

- Transitioning to higher education students paying more is essential to mitigate fiscal constraints and enhance efficiency.
- Braconier's analysis suggests that increased co-payments can be more

responsive in influencing the supply of graduates.

· Shifting funding responsibilities to students aligns incentives and generates additional resources for expanding tertiary education.

· Robust loan systems are necessary to ensure equitable access to tertiary
education during this transition.

6. International Impacts of Education Policies and Inequality Challenges:

· International repercussions of education policies occur through migration
patterns and trade dynamics.

· Slower human capital growth in certain emerging economies affects
global GDP, trade patterns, and migration.

· Addressing skill-biased technological change (SBTC) and income inequality requires careful policy trade-offs.

· Tax and transfer systems can mitigate the impact of market earnings on
household disposable income.

Enhancing National Policies for Technological Advancement

National policies are crucial in maximizing the benefits of faster technological change. By promoting the accumulation of Knowledge-Based Capital
(KBC), effective competition and innovation policies can encourage additional
investments in skills, capital, and organizational changes. The ability of organizations to restructure is vital for leveraging the benefits of new technologies.
For instance, to maximize the potential of Information and Communication
Technology (ICT), firms must integrate ICT into a comprehensive system
of mutually reinforcing organizational changes. Enabling factors, such as
managerial quality and private sector Research and Development (R&D),
are essential for adapting to changes at the technological frontier. Global
integration intensifies the importance of enabling factors for countries'
growth prospects, irrespective of the pace of frontier growth. Government

policies that foster strong management practices, such as reducing Product Market Regulations (PMR), can significantly impact a country's ability to benefit from positive shocks to the growth of frontier technologies. The quality of managerial capital influences a country's ability to capitalize on discoveries.

A country's capacity to benefit from technological advancements is closely tied to its domestic R&D efforts. Higher R&D spending can yield productivity benefits by stimulating innovation and enabling the imitation of others' discoveries. Structural policies, including business R&D, are crucial for encouraging Knowledge-Based Capital investment. Innovation-specific policies like R&D tax incentives and direct government support are associated with increased business R&D spending. The long-run growth model might underestimate GDP per capita in countries with high absorptive capacity, as it does not incorporate channels related to managerial quality and business R&D. For instance, countries with high managerial quality and substantial business R&D spending may experience additional increases in GDP per capita by 2060 when considering the role of these enabling factors, which underscores the need for a holistic approach to shaping national policies to ensure optimal benefits from technological advancements.

Adapting Labor and Education Policies to Changing Demographics and Skill Demands

In response to changing demographics and increasing skill requirements, labor and education policies must undergo adjustments to sustain economic growth. Addressing the challenges posed by unfavorable demographics involves implementing retirement reforms and fostering immigration-friendly policies. Even with adjustments to the retirement age for increased longevity, many countries are expected to face a decline in labor supply and slower growth. Retirement reforms, comprising two phases, aim to raise labor force participation and employment will have to be implemented in many countries. The retirement age, currently 65 years in many countries, may need to be raised to 70 and 75 years to maintain the share of active lives amidst increasing life expectancy, which is projected to result in a total average increase of 2.4 percentage points in labor force participation rates by 2060. Bridging the gap between legislated and necessary reforms requires proactive communication and strategic sequencing to overcome potential political obstacles.

Simultaneously, policymakers in OECD countries cannot rely solely on migration inflows to alleviate demographic challenges, as wage convergence between OECD and non-OECD countries might diminish incentives for work-related migration. Consequently, OECD nations may need more migration-friendly policies to attract labor. While traditional migration policies have only sometimes achieved their intended goals, well-designed government programs targeting specific types of workers could prove effective. Different immigration policies, such as skills-based point systems, family reunification programs, refugee policies, and policies addressing illegal immigration, can be tailored to attract diverse migrant groups. Changes in one country's policies may also have spillover effects on other regions, emphasizing the need for coordinated efforts.

Moreover, creating a conducive structural policy environment can attract inward migration and optimize immigration benefits, including providing migrants with h access to employment opportunities and facilitating entrepreneurship. Less restrictive business regulations positively correlate with immigration, highlighting the importance of well-functioning labor markets, especially for immigrants who may be formally overqualified for their jobs compared to the native population.

Addressing Labor Market Dynamics in the Context of Evolving Demand and an Aging Workforce

As the structure of labor demand undergoes changes influenced by economic growth, technological advancements, and evolving specialization patterns, a critical focus on flexibility and effective matching becomes imperative. The dynamic interplay of these factors generates shifts in labor demand structures, with the pace of structural change potentially fluctuating over the next 50 years. While some experts anticipate a slowdown, particularly in emerging economies transitioning from primary production, unforeseen shocks and shifts in demand patterns could significantly impact future developments. Structural changes will persist within sectors, propelled by knowledge-based growth leading to substantial firm turnover. Over the next six decades, labor forces will significantly age due to population composition and anticipated increases in retirement ages.

The aging workforce challenges labor supply dynamics by diminishing risk-taking, flexibility, and geographic mobility. This shift demands nuanced policy responses:

Adapting Active Labor Market Policies: With a rising median age in the workforce, active labor market policies need restructuring. Younger workers, often experiencing brief spells of unemployment, require a focus on search activities. Conversely, older workers facing longer unemployment periods and higher exit risks may necessitate a stronger emphasis on maintaining general skills and lowering reservation wages.

Extended Working Careers and Skill Requirements: As working careers lengthen and skill demands rise, there is a growing need for on-the-job and out-of-job retraining. The extended period of skill depreciation and the risk of human capital obsolescence due to technological changes highlight the importance of continuous skill development throughout longer working lives.

Enhancing Labor-Market Matching: Complementary measures can improve labor-market matching alongside activation policies. Lowering employment protection, particularly on permanent contracts, may encourage employers to hire workers with evolving skills, anticipating skill development on the job.

This approach recognizes that labor market experience and exposure to appropriately challenging tasks contribute to skill maintenance and development, while underutilization may accelerate skill depreciation.

Shaping Education Policies in Response to Growing Skill Demands

The escalating Demand for skills in the era of knowledge-based growth necessitates a strategic reevaluation of education policies. As skill requirements evolve due to skill-biased technical advancements, shifting specialization patterns, and changing demand compositions, educational policies become pivotal in steering overall growth. However, achieving substantial increases in educational attainment and skills encounters notable challenges:

Focus on Early Education Quality: Acknowledging the high social returns to education, particularly in earlier stages and for disadvantaged individuals, emphasizes the importance of enhancing the quality of primary and secondary education across diverse population segments, which not only ensures improved productivity but also facilitates increased participation in higher education. Prioritizing high-quality primary and secondary education becomes a prerequisite for elevating skill levels and expanding tertiary education, warranting prioritized public funding.

Adapting to Longer Working Lives: While extended working lives to heighten incentives for educational investment, they also elevate the risk of acquired education and skills becoming obsolete. Consequently, there is a growing need for a stronger emphasis on life-long learning. Government support for life-long learning gains significance, particularly for older workers with lower cross-country mobility, ensuring the social benefits translate into higher productivity and longer careers domestically.

Financial Considerations for Higher Education: Given fiscal constraints and increased international mobility of skilled labor, introducing co-payments for higher education becomes an attractive option. Private benefits from higher education are anticipated to remain high due to the rising Demand for skilled labor. Addressing the expected surge in Demand for tertiary education may strain public budgets significantly unless alternative funding sources or cost-effective study arrangements are explored. As outlined earlier, a government-funded expansion aligned with the central scenario's higher Demand for tertiary graduations could elevate public spending by approximately 1% of GDP in the average OECD country if spending per student remains constant. The prospect of larger co-payments by students emerges as a potential solution in response to these financial pressures, with considerations for such adjustments intensifying across the OECD.

Switching to Loan Funding Models for Tertiary Education

Many countries would need to consider transitioning towards having higher education students pay more for education, which is so for several reasons:

Mitigating Fiscal Constraints: Without such a shift, fiscal limitations may impede funding for tertiary education, leading to either a stagnant supply of graduate study opportunities or diminishing funding per student. This scenario could hinder overall growth and exacerbate earning disparities compared to the central scenario.

Efficiency Gains: Braconier (2014) reveals that the supply of graduates is notably more responsive to increasing co-payments than to augmented funding from government or corporate sources. As technological progress may slow with convergence and reduced structural change, skill requirements might escalate less rapidly than in recent decades, providing an efficient rationale for higher student co-payments.

Educational Performance Impact: Braconier's analysis indicates that enhanced educational performance in secondary schooling, as measured by PISA scores, amplifies the Demand for education and boosts the supply of tertiary education. Higher-quality entrants into tertiary education tend to progress more smoothly, exhibit lower dropout rates, and positively influence their peers' ability to advance.

Internationalization and Mobility: The rising internationalization of higher education and increased mobility of skilled labor strengthens the rationale for students to shoulder a larger share of tertiary education costs, which aligns with the trend of a growing number of OECD students enrolled abroad.

Alignment of Incentives: Shifting funding responsibilities to students could better align incentives and generate additional resources for expanding tertiary education. However, this transition necessitates the development of robust loan systems to ensure equitable access to tertiary education.

Insurance Against Risk: Loan systems with repayments contingent on income can offer insurance against risks associated with educational investments, which is particularly relevant as within-class and within-occupation wage dispersion has increased, suggesting a rise in risks related to educational investments.

Evolution of Education Production: While funding reforms are crucial for enhancing educational attainment, the evolving landscape of training and studying methods may dramatically change the production of higher education in the next 50 years. The proliferation of online courses, such as Massive Online Open Courses (MOOCs), indicates avenues to increase availability and participation at a lower cost, challenging the traditional face-to-face interaction model. The extent to which these new methods can replace traditional education remains an open question.

International Impacts of Education Policies and Inequality Challenges

Education Policy Spillovers: International repercussions of national education policies are primarily channeled through migration patterns and trade dynamics. Recent OECD research examining the global effects of slower human capital growth in China, India, and Indonesia indicates potential reductions in real GDP by 2060 for these countries.

Trade Spillovers: The impact of slower educational advancement in emerging economies is transmitted globally via altered specialization patterns. Less skill upgrading influences relative wages, particularly favoring skilled labor, and hinders the specialization process in human capital-intensive sectors. This effect allows OECD economies to maintain their comparative advantage, particularly in electronics and services. However, the influence on trading partners' wages appears minimal.

Migration Patterns: Elevated relative wages for skilled labor in China, India, and Indonesia affect migration flows towards the OECD. The analysis by Westmore (2014) suggests a slowdown in the migration of skilled workers due to less ambitious education policies in emerging economies, while less-skilled migration increases. By 2060, this shift could lead to a 0.4 percent reduction in the US stock of skilled migrants and a corresponding increase in less-skilled migrants. The Netherlands could experience a 1.8 percent decrease and a 2.8 percent increase.

Addressing Inequality and Social Pressures

Skill-Biased Technological Change (SBTC): The prominence of a knowledge-based economy will amplify the value of skills. Skill-biased technological change (SBTC) remains a driving force behind increasing income inequality. Attempts to curb SBTC are challenging, given its correlation with multifactor productivity growth and the global nature of this trend through trade.

Policy Instruments and Trade-Offs: Policy instruments aimed at reducing earning inequality sometimes pose challenges to growth. The central scenario anticipates a 10% reduction in earning inequality through increased educational attainment by 2060. However, achieving further reductions would require highly ambitious educational scaling. Structural reforms, reversing trends contributing to earning inequality, may lessen the baseline increase by half. However, these reforms may adversely impact growth due to product market regulation and wage-related effects.

Trade-Offs Between Income Distribution and Growth: Trade-offs between household disposable income and growth become evident in the influence of policies on gross wage effects, employment effects, and net tax and benefit effects. Policy impacts on labor market patterns and tax systems contribute to diverging developments in gross earnings and household disposable incomes. Differential impacts of structural reforms on earnings inequality and employment necessitate careful policy trade-offs. Pro-employment policies, such as reducing gaps in employment protection, offer avenues with less severe trade-offs while combining reforms with conditionality can mitigate negative effects.

Tax and Transfer Systems' Impact on Income Distribution

Tax and transfer systems traditionally alleviate the impact of changes in market earnings on household disposable income. However, the effectiveness of these systems has diminished over the past decades due to reduced redistributive measures in the OECD area. Despite being more impactful in countries with higher pre-tax income inequality, considerable variation in their effectiveness is primarily attributed to the redistributive impact of transfers, highlighting the potential for enhancing targeted tax and benefit systems to mitigate the growing impact of market income inequality on household income dispersion across many countries. Well-designed social benefit systems offer ex-ante risk insurance and address moral hazard and incentive issues through conditionality.

Global Integration Challenges and the Growth-Equity Trade-Off

Increasing global integration and the competition for mobile skilled workers may jeopardize the economic feasibility of certain redistribution instruments. This scenario could lead to an institutional "race to the bottom." The simultaneous rise in the Demand for redistribution, driven by increasing earning differentials, and the costs associated with redistribution present a heightened growth-equity trade-off for national policymakers. Addressing this challenge can be approached through three avenues:

1. a focus on increasing equality of opportunity, such as educational reforms
2. shifting taxes from mobile to less mobile tax bases
3. enhancing international coordination of tax policies

The anticipated "race to the bottom" is not an assured outcome of further global integration and skill-biased technological change (SBTC). Labor market and social institutions provide income insurance against various risks, and evidence suggests that global integration has not significantly influenced the extent of social and labor market reforms. Furthermore, the expected growth of emerging economies is likely to result in more developed labor market institutions and increased social spending in these regions.

Policies to Address Climate Change

Mitigating Climate Change: Effectively addressing climate change involves a balanced set of policies focusing on emission reduction and adaptation. Mitigation strategies should incorporate appropriate carbon pricing and targeted measures like reforming fossil-fuel subsidies, regulatory changes, increased R&D investment, and market reforms in energy and transportation.

Impact of Trade Integration on Emission Location: The downside of rising trade integration may be increased sensitivity of emission-intensive production to energy prices, potentially leading to tax and subsidy competition and excessive emissions. Alternative mechanisms like border carbon adjustments may become necessary without a binding multilateral agreement. However, the challenges and costs of implementing such measures emphasize the need for a globally coordinated solution. Regional cooperation through plurilateral linking of carbon markets can help mitigate the effects of carbon emissions "leakage."

Environmental-Friendly Energy Transition: Transitioning to environmentally friendly energy sources could reduce climate change damages and enhance global welfare. However, this may require substantial initial upfront investments.

Costs and Urgency of Climate Change Action: The full costs of climate change will extend beyond 2060, with significant impacts anticipated by that time. The inertia in polluting production systems and atmospheric greenhouse gas concentrations introduces risks of threshold effects triggering major negative events. Urgent policy action is imperative for both mitigation and adaptation.

Policy Mix for Climate Change Mitigation: A comprehensive policy mix is essential for mitigating climate change. Carbon pricing, coupled with targeted measures like reforming fossil-fuel subsidies, energy efficiency standards, increased R&D, energy market regulation reforms, and information-based policies, can address environmental damages and generate substantial fiscal revenues.

International Cooperation for Global Climate Challenges: Given the global consequences of climate change, a cooperative policy solution is crucial. Efforts are underway through the UN for a global agreement in 2015, acknowledging the challenges of cooperation due to varying costs and benefits across countries. The convergence in per capita income over the next 50 years might ease coordination, but the diverse economic impacts of climate change pose potential hindrances.

Enhancing Coordination for Climate Action

The coordination challenge in addressing climate change may intensify with further reductions in trade costs. This reduction can render the localization of high-emission activities more sensitive to local costs, potentially discouraging countries from imposing higher carbon prices. Without reinforced international cooperation on emissions reduction at the multilateral level, there is a growing push for alternative mechanisms like border carbon adjustments despite the practical challenges associated with their implementation (Cosbey, 2008). The potential expenses of such measures should serve as a compelling incentive to seek a globally coordinated solution. Meanwhile, regional collaboration, such as plurilateral linking of carbon markets, can help mitigate the impacts of carbon emissions "leakage."

Climate Change and Production Costs: Changing climatic conditions will impact relative production costs, influencing countries' comparative advantages. For instance, a climate change-induced decline in agricultural production in Southeast Asia could subtract approximately 1.7 percent from the region's GDP by 2060. While further global trade integration can reduce the costs of adapting to climate change by facilitating shifts in specialization patterns and global adaptation, it is important to note that international trade also contributes to emissions.

Uncertainties in Global Climate Change Damages: Estimates of global climate change damages are surrounded by uncertainties, with even greater uncertainty in the distribution of regional damages. The risks of more dramatic regional developments within the next 50 years are substantial, bringing associated costs such as disrupted food supply, lost output, and environmental migration pressures. Given the high uncertainty surrounding regional impacts, mechanisms for global risk-sharing could prove valuable. While trade integration offers one such mechanism, further financial integration could enhance risk sharing, especially in terms of long-term investment.

Investment Requirements for Climate Action: Effective climate change mitigation demands significant investment in developing new technologies, enhancing the uptake of existing technologies, and fostering greener energy systems. Similarly, climate change will necessitate substantial investments in adaptation, particularly considering that some damages from climate change are likely already "locked in." Enabling pension funds to invest more freely across borders could provide additional sources for long-term investment in mitigation and adaptation without jeopardizing macroeconomic balances.

Addressing Fiscal Challenges through Strategic Policies

The fiscal challenges arising from gaps and spending on health, pensions, education, and migration are anticipated to reach 10 percent of GDP in 2060 for the average OECD country. Relying solely on fiscal consolidation to tackle these issues would significantly diminish growth and equity. Therefore, a shift towards structural reforms that reduce dependence on public funding and strengthen fiscal is essential. The key aspects for consideration are articulated further below:

Pension System Transformation: Embracing defined-contribution pension systems can enhance fiscal resilience amid uncertainties in demographics and productivity. However, this shift would transfer more risks to participants, necessitating a careful balance.

Global Tax Coordination: Strengthening global tax coordination, particularly in areas with substantial negative externalities like carbon taxation, is advantageous. This coordination can improve efficiency and generate additional revenues, with benefits growing alongside continued global integration.

Adapting to Tax Base Mobility: As global integration progresses, certain tax bases become more mobile. To counteract rising tax competition and preserve environmental and corporate taxes, a viable option is to shift taxation towards less mobile bases such as property and resources.

Challenges in Fiscal Consolidation Tools: Recent OECD analysis highlights that various fiscal consolidation tools involve trade-offs with growth, equity, and current account imbalances, particularly in the short term. The choice of consolidation instruments depends on the scale of needed consolidation, national preferences for income versus equity, and the relative efficacy of these instruments.

Structural reforms can help achieve the following:

1. Mitigating Fiscal Pressures: Structural reforms can alleviate fiscal pressures without compromising growth and equity. Adjusting the retirement age based on increasing life expectancy and relying more on tuition fees for tertiary education are examples where positive side effects on growth and equity can be achieved through careful implementation.

2. Managing Risks: Structural reforms contribute to the resilience of public finances against unforeseen developments and shocks. State-dependent policies, such as automatic longevity adjustments and balancing mechanisms, enhance fiscal resilience. However, these policies must fully resolve the trade-off between sustainability, adequacy, and efficiency in social protection systems.

3. Private Funding in Key Areas: Greater reliance on private funds can be considered, especially in financing infrastructure or long-term care. This approach diversifies funding sources and contributes to fiscal sustainability.

4. Capital Allocation and Labor Mobility: Policies enabling pension funds

to invest globally improve capital allocation, generating returns and risk-sharing benefits. Facilitating the portability of worker pension benefits enhances labor allocation to regions facing chronic shortages and attracts foreign workers.

In summary, strategic structural reforms offer a nuanced approach to addressing fiscal challenges, balancing the need for sustainability, growth, and equity.

Review Questions

1. How do government policies, such as reducing Product Market Regulations, impact a country's ability to benefit from technological advancements?
2. What are the challenges and considerations in implementing retirement reforms, including raising the retirement age to 70-75?
3. How can active labor market policies be adapted to cater to the needs of younger and older workers in the face of evolving Demand?
4. What role do primary and secondary education play in shaping skill levels and participation in higher education?
5. Discuss the potential benefits and challenges of transitioning to loan funding models for tertiary education.
6. How do international education policies influence migration patterns, trade dynamics, and global GDP?

Discussion Points

1. Explore the potential trade-offs between policies to reduce income inequality and their impact on economic growth.
2. Discuss the role of online education and Massive Online Open Courses (MOOCs) in reshaping the traditional education landscape.Analyze the implications of increasing global integration on the feasibility of certain redistribution instruments and potential "race to the bottom" scenarios

CHAPTER SEVEN: STRATEGIC FISCAL AND MACROECONOMIC POLICIES AND GLOBAL ECONOMIC SHIFTS

Summary of Key Points

1. Adapting Fiscal Instruments to Global Integration:

   - Global integration increases mobility, challenging traditional fiscal instruments and impacting tax efficiency.
   - Tax competition risks driving rates below optimal levels, necessitating international tax coordination.
   - Changes in the efficiency of fiscal instruments vary based on income levels and inequality trends among countries.

2. Policies for Addressing Global Challenges in a Shifting Landscape:

   - Structural policy instruments can prevent medium-term current account imbalances, addressing labor market reforms and financial liberalization.
   - Economic policies emphasizing productivity, equity, and robust public finances are crucial in a changing world.
   - Global integration and knowledge-based growth demand international cooperation in research, intellectual property, and greenhouse gas taxation.

3. Enhancing Risk-Sharing and Fiscal Strategies in a Globalized Economy:

- Trade and long-term investment integration play vital roles in climate risk mitigation and bolstering risk-sharing mechanisms.
- Fiscal strategies must include consolidation efforts, structural reforms, and adaptation to global taxation challenges.
- Global coordination on taxation is essential for fortifying fiscal positions and fostering equity amid changing economic dynamics.

Adapting Fiscal Instruments to Global Integration

Over the next fifty years, the hierarchy of fiscal instruments may transform due to evolving economic structures and rising global integration. The increased mobility of capital and production across borders is expected to elevate the costs of taxing these sources, particularly regarding efficiency losses. Additionally, the growing significance of knowledge-based assets and multinational enterprises on a global scale is likely to impact governments' ability to collect taxes, diminishing the efficiency of corporate income taxes and production-oriented environmental taxes at the national level. The following implications for tax competition and coordination are pertinent:

Tax Competition Challenges: The risk of tax competition potentially driving down rates below optimal levels underscores the importance of international tax coordination, which is particularly relevant for corporate income taxes and environmental taxes tied to production.

Gains from International Tax Coordination: Coordinated action on environmental issues can yield substantial fiscal revenues. Broad international coordination is essential to prevent leakages that may occur with limited participation.

Country-Specific Considerations: Changes in the ranking of fiscal instruments will vary among countries based on income levels and inequality trends. Countries experiencing above-average increases in incomes and inequality may prioritize fiscal instruments with lower impacts on inequality. Conversely, countries anticipating below-average increases may emphasize growth-enhancing fiscal instruments.

The following macroeconomic stability strategies are recommended:

Shared Domestic Shocks: With increasing economic integration, the impact of domestic shocks will be shared with trading partners, reducing the need for standalone stabilization policies and prompting a shift towards cooperative stabilization policies, necessitating concerted efforts in deficit and surplus countries to avoid current account imbalances.

Policy Interdependence: Trade and investment integration creates economic and policy interdependence among partner countries. The rise in international spillovers from demand and supply shocks emphasizes the need for stronger international coordination on fiscal and structural policies.

Risk-Sharing and Coordination: More intertwined economies result in increased risk-sharing, necessitating coordination on stabilization and structural policies. Close trade partners, such as within the EU, may benefit from deeper coordination. At the same time, OECD countries need to develop coordination with emerging economies as their importance in the global economy grows.

Stabilizing Impact of Integration: Deeper integration is expected to stabilize economies and synchronize business cycles. However, with rising exposure to emerging economies, OECD countries may experience a more muted stabilizing effect. As cross-border trade increases, domestic fiscal multipliers may diminish, necessitating greater international cooperation in monetary and fiscal action to address synchronized business cycles effectively.

In summary, adapting fiscal instruments to the challenges and opportunities presented by global integration requires a nuanced approach that considers national priorities and international coordination efforts.

Policies for Addressing Global Challenges in a Shifting Landscape

Managing Current Account Imbalances: Efficient use of structural policy instruments can prevent the reoccurrence of current account imbalances in the medium term. Key measures include:

1. Labor market reforms in euro area deficit countries and Japan.
2. Product market reforms in euro area surplus countries.
3. Less favorable tax treatment of interest expenses in the United States.
4. Financial liberalization and expanding social safety nets in China.

Additionally, demographic factors and fiscal policies will play a role in driving long-term current account imbalances. Policymakers must address large imbalances and mitigate the risks of these imbalances leading to future macroeconomic crises. Factors such as the composition of international financial linkages become crucial, focusing on reducing risks associated with short-term foreign currency borrowing.

Economic Policies for a Changing World: Policies enhancing productivity, supporting equity, maintaining robust public finances, and discouraging the overuse of natural resources remain crucial. The need to strengthen economic and political institutions persists.

Global Integration and Knowledge-Based Growth

Further global integration and the reliance on knowledge-based assets necessitate international coordination for global public goods. The following possible areas of cooperation are pertinent:

1. Cooperation on basic research, intellectual property rights, competition regulation, and enforcement can enhance growth.
2. International collaboration on taxing greenhouse gas emissions becomes more critical with rising trade integration.

Flexible Markets for Growth and Equity: Flexible product and labor markets are vital for faster technology absorption and lower structural adjustment costs. However, the relevant policies should be pursued cautiously to minimize potential negative impacts on equity.

Education and Skilled Labor Mobility: Private and social returns to education are expected to rise, contributing to stronger growth and lower inequality. Enhancing focus on pre-tertiary education and life-long learning is important in the face of fiscal constraints and limited international labor mobility. Tuition-based and loan-financed tertiary education may offer efficiency benefits in a world with high skilled labor mobility.

Equity Enhancement and Labor Market Functioning

Mitigating Skill-Biased Technological Change: As technological progress remains skill-biased, structural policies focusing on pre-tax earnings may be costly in growth terms. Emphasizing policies that enhance equal opportunities, especially in education, can address this dilemma.

Structural Change and Workforce Flexibility: Structural change may slow in OECD economies while emerging economies initially experience higher rates of change. The workforce's flexibility will decline in both regions, emphasizing the need for adaptable labor market policies focusing on training and lowering reservation wages.

Climate Change Mitigation

Front-Loaded Action and Carbon Pricing: The economic costs of climate change are anticipated to be significant by 2060, emphasizing the need for prompt action. Carbon pricing, requiring international coordination, is crucial to discourage emissions.

Challenges in Emission-Intensive Taxation: Global trade and investment integration will render production-based taxes on emission-intensive activities less efficient. The absence of a binding multilateral agreement necessitates a coordinated global solution over alternative mechanisms like border carbon adjustments.

In summary, navigating the evolving economic landscape demands strategic policymaking that addresses current challenges while anticipating future shifts. Policymakers must balance growth, equity, and environmental concerns through international collaboration and forward-thinking measures.

Enhancing Risk-Sharing and Fiscal Strategies in a Globalized Economy

Trade and Investment Integration for Climate Risk Mitigation: Trade and long-term investment integration play pivotal roles in bolstering risk-sharing mechanisms, particularly in the face of unpredictable climate damage.

Fiscal and Macroeconomic Strategies: The next fifty years pose substantial fiscal challenges and risks, necessitating a multifaceted approach:

Consolidation and Structural Reforms: Essential consolidation efforts must be complemented by structural reforms aimed at cost savings (e.g., in education) and fortifying the resilience of public finances (e.g., pension systems) against shocks like migration.

Taxation Adaptation to Global Integration: Increasing global integration, coupled with the growing significance of mobile intangible inputs in economic growth, amplifies the social costs of taxing capital and other mobile factors within a single country. A strategic shift towards taxing more immobile bases becomes imperative to align with the evolving economic landscape.

Global Coordination on Taxation: Advocating for global coordination on taxation emerges as a supportive measure for fortifying fiscal positions and fostering equity amid the changing economic dynamics.

Shared Domestic Shocks and Macroeconomic Coordination: The trend of rising global integration implies that domestic shocks will be increasingly shared with trade partners. While average volatility may decline, the efficacy of fiscal policies in stabilization will diminish. Consequently, the benefits of macroeconomic coordination are poised to increase, given the intertwined nature of the global economy.

Cross-Border Long-Term Investment Integration: Emphasizing the importance of cross-border long-term investment integration to enhance risk-sharing mechanisms and mitigate the risks of sudden reversals due to current account imbalances.

In summary, navigating the challenges and opportunities of the evolving global economic landscape requires strategic fiscal and macroeconomic policies. From adapting taxation approaches to global integration to fostering international coordination, policymakers must proactively address the multifaceted dimensions of the changing economic environment.

Review Questions

1. How does increased global integration impact the efficiency of traditional fiscal instruments, especially in taxing capital and production-oriented environmental taxes?
2. Discuss the risks associated with tax competition and the importance of international tax coordination in preventing suboptimal tax rates.
3. How do changes in the ranking of fiscal instruments vary among countries based on income levels and inequality trends?
4. What structural policy measures are recommended to prevent the reoccurrence of current account imbalances in the medium term?
5. How can policymakers balance growth, equity, and environmental concerns through international collaboration in a changing economic landscape?
6. Explain the challenges and opportunities associated with adapting taxation approaches to global integration.

Discussion Points

1. Explore the potential implications of shared domestic shocks in the context of increasing economic integration and the need for macroeconomic coordination.
2. Discuss the role of cross-border long-term investment integration in

enhancing risk-sharing mechanisms and mitigating risks associated with sudden reversals due to current account imbalances.

3. Analyze the trade-offs between economic policies emphasizing productivity and equity, considering potential impacts on growth and income distribution.

4. Debate the challenges and benefits of global coordination on taxation, especially in the context of diverse economic structures and priorities among countries.

5. Discuss the role of fiscal strategies in addressing climate change challenges, particularly the importance of carbon pricing and global cooperation in emission-intensive taxation.

6. Explore the implications of knowledge-based growth on international cooperation in research, intellectual property rights, and technology transfer.

CONCLUSION

The book "Fiscal Dynamics in a Transforming Global Economy" explores the realms of public finance, monetary policy, the future landscape, and strategic reforms shaping our complex and fast-evolving world. The seven chapters of this book unveil the foundational principles that define public finance, its historical evolution, and attempts to project the fiscal dynamics in a fast-evolving world. The book scrutinized the challenges and opportunities presented by global transformations, projecting into a future where strategic fiscal reforms are indispensable for sustainable, knowledge-based growth. Like interconnected pieces of a puzzle, the chapters contribute to a holistic understanding of the dynamic forces at play in the global economic arena. The book underscores the critical role fiscal policies play in fostering economic stability, promoting equity, and ensuring the long-term sustainability of nations.

As we gaze into the future, the challenges of fiscal consolidation, demographic shifts, and the uncertainties surrounding productivity and education dynamics beckon us to reflect on the adaptability and resilience of national policies. The strategic structural reforms outlined underscore the necessity of embracing technological advancement while fostering equitable growth. The final chapter widens attempts to encapsulate the global shifts and the role of fiscal instruments in a rapidly integrating world, calling for international cooperation, risk-sharing mechanisms, and the fortification of fiscal positions for the optimal success of fiscal policies in a globalized economy.

Fiscal Dynamics in a Transforming Global Economy empowers readers with insights that transcend the boundaries of conventional economic discourse. It recognizes that fiscal dynamics are not static but adaptive, not fixed but evolving, and echoes in the ongoing conversations, policy decisions, and collective efforts to navigate the transformative currents of policymaking in a fast-changing global economy. May the wisdom distilled within these chapters serve as a guiding compass for those shaping the economic destinies of nations. The future awaits, and with it, the responsibility to craft fiscal policies that resonate with the pulse of a transforming global economy.

SOURCES

Fiscal Policy for Economic Development: An Overview Benedict Clements, Sanjeev Gupta, And Gabriela Inchauste https://www.imf.org/external/pubs/nft/2004/hcd/ch01.pdf

Chapter 23 - Environmental Taxation and Regulation A. Lans Bovenberg, Lawrence H. Goulder https://www.sciencedirect.com/science/article/abs/pii/S1573442002800271

Chapter 32 - What is a Sustainable Public Debt? P. D'Erasmo E.G. Mendoza J. Zhang https://www.sciencedirect.com/science/article/abs/pii/S1574004816000148

All About Fiscal Policy: What It Is, Why It Matters, and Examples https://www.investopedia.com/terms/f/fiscalpolicy.asp

"Fiscal Policy" Before Keynes' General Theory Marianne Johnson file:///C:/Users/USER/Downloads/SSRN-id3252526.pdf

Fiscal Policy: Taking and Giving Away Mark Horton, Asmaa El-Ganainy https://www.imf.org/en/Publications/fandd/issues/Series/Back-to-Basics/Fiscal-Policy

Expansionary and Contractionary Fiscal Policy https://courses.lumenlearning.com/wm-macroeconomics/chapter/expansionary-and-contractionary-fiscal-policy/

Expansionary Fiscal Policy: Risks and Examples https://www.investopedia.com/terms/e/expansionary_policy.asp

Monetary Policy vs. Fiscal Policy: What's the Difference? https://www.investopedia.com/ask/answers/100314/whats-difference-between-monetary-policy-and-fiscal-policy.asp

How fiscal policy impacts business https://gocardless.com/guides/posts/how-fiscal-policy-impacts-business/

Fiscal Policy: Economic Effects Jeffrey M. Stupak Analyst in Macroeconomic Policy file:///C:/Users/USER/Documents/public%20finance/20190516_.pdf

Tax and Fiscal Policy in Response to the Coronavirus Crisis: Strengthening Confidence and Resilience https://read.oecd-ilibrary.org/view/?ref=128_128575-o6raktcoaa&title=Tax-and-Fiscal-Policy-in-Response-to-the-Coronavirus-Crisis

Fiscal policy and high inflation https://www.ecb.europa.eu/pub/economic-bulletin/articles/2023/html/ecb.ebart202302_01~2bd46eff8f.en.html

All About Fiscal Policy: What It Is, Why It Matters, and Examples ADAM HAYES https://www.investopedia.com/terms/f/fiscalpolicy.asp

A Monetary and Fiscal History of the United States, 1961-2022 alan blinder https://www.milkenreview.org/articles/a-monetary-and-fiscal-history-of-the-united-states-1961-2022

Interactions between fiscal and monetary policies: a brief history of a long relationship https://www.pse-journal.hr/en/archive/interactions-between-fiscal-and-monetary-policies-a-brief-history-of-a-long-relationship_7902/

Taxation https://www.britannica.com/money/topic/taxation

Chapter 2 Fundamental principles of taxation https://www.oecd-ilibrary.org/docserver/9789264218789-5-en.pdf?e=1703964323&id=id&accname=guest&checksum=91EDD7C1544E5D4777ECE5A320702571

The Theoretical Foundations of Regulation on Public Finances http://real.mtak.hu/146408/1/CEALSCEPhD02RegulationofPublicFinances2.pdf

Public Finance: Theory and Practice in the Central European Transition https://www.nispa.org/files/publications/ebooks/Public-Finance-Theory-and-Practice.pdf

What Are Public Goods? Definition, How They Work, and Example JASON FERNANDO https://www.investopedia.com/terms/p/public-good.asp

Public Goods https://courses.lumenlearning.com/wm-microeconomics/chapter/public-goods/

The rationale for public sector intervention in the economy https://www.london.gov.uk/sites/default/files/gla_migrate_files_destination/rationale_for_public_sector_intervention.pdf

Free Rider Benefiting from a common resource without paying for it https://corporatefinanceinstitute.com/resources/economics/free-rider/

Free-rider problem https://en.wikipedia.org/wiki/Free-rider_problem#:~:text=In%20the%20social%20sciences%2C%20the,goods%20of%20a%20communal%20nature

The advantage of international fiscal cooperation under alternative monetary regimes https://www.sciencedirect.com/science/article/abs/pii/S0176268096000122

Who benefits from international fiscal cooperation? The role of cross-country asymmetries George Liontos a, Apostolis Philippopoulos https://www.sciencedirect.com/science/article/abs/pii/S1703494923000026

International tax cooperation and capital mobility https://repositorio.cepal.org/server/api/core/bitstreams/e4d0935a-6ae8-4ba7-8430-c7601f8cb058/content

Case Studies of Fiscal Councils—Functions and Impact https://www.imf.org/external/np/pp/eng/2013/071613a.pdf

Chapter 7 Broader tax challenges raised by the digital economy https://www.oecd-ilibrary.org/docserver/9789264218789-10-en.pdf?expires=1703975653&id=id&accname=guest&checksum=410D401BCAC2A4DD84E56FC0ED2A1892

Taxing the Digital Economy in Latin America and the Caribbean: What can be done https://www.afronomicslaw.org/2020/12/09/taxing-the-digital-economy-in-latin-america-and-the-caribbean-what-can-be-done

Green Fiscal Reforms, Environment and Sustainable Development https://onlineacademicpress.com/index.php/IJAEFA/article/view/6/375

What Are Smart Contracts on the Blockchain and How They Work https://www.investopedia.com/terms/s/smart-contracts.asp

Aging Populations and
Public Pension Schemes https://www.imf.org/external/pubs/nft/op/147/

Fiscal Policy David N. Weil https://www.econlib.org/library/Enc/FiscalPoli

cy.html

Do Enlarged Fiscal Deficits Cause Inflation: The Historical Record Michael D. Bordo Mickey D. Levy Working Paper 28195 https://www.nber.org/system/files/working_papers/w28195/w28195.pdf

Fiscal Policy Can Help Tame Inflation and Protect the Most Vulnerable https://www.imf.org/en/Blogs/Articles/2023/04/03/fiscal-policy-can-help-tame-inflation-and-protect-the-most-vulnerable

Public Policy Origins, Practice, and Analysis https://web.ung.edu/media/university-press/public-policy.pdf?t=1661449833017

What are the principles of good taxation? https://www.futurelearn.com/info/courses/public-financial-management/0/steps/14705#:~:text=The%20principles%20of%20good%20taxation%20were%20formulated%20many%20years%20ago,%2C%20certainty%2C%20convenience%20and%20efficiency

Principles of Taxation https://taxjustice-and-poverty.org/fileadmin/Dateien/Taxjustice_and_Poverty/Introduction/05_Principles.pdf

Taxes Definition: Type, Who Pays and Why https://www.investopedia.com/terms/t/taxes.asp

Classes of taxes https://www.britannica.com/money/topic/taxation/Classes-of-taxes

Analysis of Assessment Methods of Tax Burden: Theoretical Aspect file:///C:/Users/USER/Downloads/2089-Article%20Text-6378-1-10-20120807.pdf

Tax shift https://en.wikipedia.org/wiki/Tax_shift#:~:text=Tax%20shift%20is%20a%20kind,the%20redistribution%20of%20tax%20burden

Distributional effects https://en.wikipedia.org/wiki/Distributional_effects#:~:text=A%20distributional%20effect%20is%20the,cost%20allocations%20of%20a%20project

Government Spending https://corporatefinanceinstitute.com/resources/economics/government-spending/

Government spending https://en.wikipedia.org/wiki/Government_spending

What Are Some Examples of Debt Instruments? https://www.investopedia.c

om/ask/answers/050515/what-are-some-examples-debt-instruments.asp

What Is a Debt Instrument? Definition, Structure, and Types https://www.investopedia.com/terms/d/debtinstrument.asp

Government Debt Management: Designing Debt Management Strategies https://thedocs.worldbank.org/en/doc/194071527797532524-0340022018/original/GDM1backgroundnotes.pdf

How to design a stimulus package https://cepr.org/voxeu/columns/how-design-stimulus-package

Green stimulus after the 2008 crisis: Learning from successes and failures https://www.iea.org/articles/green-stimulus-after-the-2008-crisis

A Comparison of Selected Stimulus Packages in 2008 and 2020: investing in Renewable Energy, Sustainable Agriculture and Food Security, and Gender Equality and the Empowerment of Women for Structural Economic transformation https://unctad.org/system/files/information-document/osg_2020-12-18_StimulusPackages_en.pdf

The United States' Response to COVID-19: A Case Study of the First Year https://globalhealthsciences.ucsf.edu/sites/globalhealthsciences.ucsf.edu/files/covid-us-case-study.pdf

China's Policy Experience in Responding to Covid-19 Shock https://unctad.org/system/files/official-document/BRI-Project_RP24_en.pdf

The Origins of Greece's Debt Crisis https://www.investopedia.com/articles/personal-finance/061115/origins-greeces-debt-crisis.asp#:~:text=The%20Greek%20debt%20crisis%20is,over%20the%20next%20thirty%20years

The IMF and the Greek Crisis: Myths and Realities

Speech by Poul Thomsen, Director of the European Department of the International Monetary Fund, at the London School of Economics https://www.imf.org/en/News/Articles/2019/10/01/sp093019-The-IMF-and-the-Greek-Crisis-Myths-and-Realities

Chapter 1. Fiscal Politics https://www.elibrary.imf.org/display/book/9781475547900/ch001.xml

Policy Challenges for the Next 50 Years https://www.oecd.org/economy/Policy-challenges-for-the-next-fifty-years.pdf

But Will It Work?: Implementation Analysis to Improve Government

Performance R. Kent Weaver https://www.brookings.edu/wp-content/upl oads/2016/06/02_implementation_analysis_weaver.pdf

Cross-Border Impacts of Fiscal Policy: Still Relevant? file:///C:/User-s/USER/Downloads/c4.pdf

What Is a Tax Treaty Between Countries & How Does It Work? https://www. investopedia.com/terms/t/taxtreaty.asp

Five common challenges with Operational Transfer Pricing https://www.d eloitte.com/global/en/services/tax/perspectives/five-common-challenges-with-operational-transfer-pricing.html

Common Transfer Pricing Issues and How to Rectify Them https://www.vi etnam-briefing.com/news/transfer-pricing-issues.html/

Regional Financial Cooperation https://repositorio.cepal.org/server/api/ core/bitstreams/c5982d1f-ee4a-464d-8e51-d199b48391b3/content

The Coordination of National Fiscal Policies in the Context of Monetary Union https://www.europarl.europa.eu/workingpapers/econ/pdf/e6en_en. pdf

ASEAN-5: Further Harnessing the Benefits of Regional Integration amid Fragmentation Risks file:///C:/Users/USER/Downloads/wpiea2023191-print-pdf.pdf

Base erosion and profit shifting https://en.wikipedia.org/wiki/Base_erosio n_and_profit_shifting#:~:text=Base%20erosion%20and%20profit%20s hifting%20(BEPS)%20refers%20to%20corporate%20tax,the%20higher% 2Dtax%20jurisdictions%20using

Cap and Trade vs Carbon Tax https://earth.org/cap-and-trade-vs-carbon-tax/#:~:text=While%20a%20carbon%20tax%20sets,the%20rise%20of%2 0global%20temperatures.

Which is better: carbon tax or cap-and-trade? https://www.lse.ac.uk/gran thaminstitute/explainers/which-is-better-carbon-tax-or-cap-and-trade/

What are some ways businesses can incentivize sustainable tourism prac-tices? https://www.linkedin.com/advice/1/what-some-ways-businesses-can-incentivize-sustainable

Practical incentives needed to help firms adopt green practices: official https://vietnamlawmagazine.vn/practical-incentives-needed-to-help-fir

ms-adopt-green-practices-official-69852.html

Green Credit Programme of India: Incentivizing Environmental Actions and Paving the Way for a Sustainable Future https://calculuscarbon.com/green-credit-programme-of-india-incentivizing-environmental-actions-and-paving-the-way-for-a-sustainable-future/

Taxing Cryptocurrencies file:///C:/Users/USER/Downloads/wpiea2023144-print-pdf%20(1).pdf

Social impact bond https://en.wikipedia.org/wiki/Social_impact_bond#:~:text=Social%20Impact%20Bonds%20(SIBs)%20are

Social Impact Bond (SIB): Definition, How It Works, and Example https://www.investopedia.com/terms/s/social-impact-bond.asp

Green Bonds And The Emergence Of Sustainable Finance In The Nigerian Capital Market https://tnp.com.ng/insights/green-bonds-and-the-emergence-of-sustainable-finance-in-the-nigerian-capital-market

Green Bond https://corporatefinanceinstitute.com/resources/esg/green-bond/

South Korea postpones 20% tax on crypto gains to 2025 https://www.forbesindia.com/article/crypto-made-easy/south-korea-postpones-20-tax-on-crypto-gains-to-2025/78341/1

The Current State of Crypto Taxation in South Korea https://www.tekedia.com/the-current-state-of-crypto-taxation-in-south-korea/

Enhancing tax transparency with blockchain technology https://punchng.com/enhancing-tax-transparency-with-blockchain-technology/#:~:text=Blockchain%20technology%20has%20the%20potential,reducing%20tax%20evasion%20and%20fraud

How we use data and analytics https://www.ato.gov.au/about-ato/commitments-and-reporting/information-and-privacy/how-we-use-data-and-analytics

Use of Big Data in Tax Administrations https://www.ciat.org/use-of-big-data-in-tax-administrations/?lang=en

Strategic tax management: best practices help ensure competitiveness https://www.dpc.com.br/strategic-tax-management-best-practices-help-ensure-competitiveness/?lang=en

7 Ways to Maximize Tax Savings with Strategic Tax Management https://www.nidhicpa.com/7-ways-to-maximize-tax-savings-with-strategic-tax-management/

What Are Tax Management Strategies? https://www.trilogyfs.com/tax-management-strategies/

Corporate Tax Planning and Financial Performance of Development Banks in Nigeria file:///C:/Users/USER/Downloads/SSRN-id3896368.pdf

Navigating the Nuances: Tax Planning with Legal Precision and Ethical Integrity https://www.linkedin.com/pulse/navigating-nuances-tax-planning-legal-precision-ethical-fdxec?trk=article-ssr-frontend-pulse_more-articles_related-content-card

Tax avoidance might be legal but it's time we seriously questioned its ethics https://www.manchester.ac.uk/discover/news/tax-avoidance-legal-ethics/

What Are Some Ways to Minimize Tax Liability? https://www.investopedia.com/ask/answers/040715/what-are-some-ways-minimize-tax-liability.asp

6 Strategies to Protect Income from Taxes https://www.investopedia.com/articles/personal-finance/032116/top-6-strategies-protect-your-income-taxes.asp

Business Taxation Meaning: Everything You Need to Know https://www.upcounsel.com/business-taxation-meaning#:~:text=of%20business%20operations.-,The%20meaning%20of%20business%20taxation%20refers%20to%20the%20taxes%20that,for%20adhering%20to%20tax%20regulations

How Does Corporate Taxation Affect Business Investment? Evidence From Aggregate and Firm-Level Data https://one.oecd.org/document/ECO/WKP(2023)18/en/pdf

Taxation of Income from Business and Investment https://www.imf.org/external/pubs/nft/1998/tlaw/eng/ch16.pdf

The Tax Advantage of Big Business: How the Structure of Corporate Taxation Fuels Concentration and Inequality https://journals.sagepub.com/doi/10.117

7/0032329220911778

Corporate Tax: Definition, Deductions, How It Works https://www.investo pedia.com/terms/c/corporatetax.asp

Determining the impact of taxation on corporate financial decision-making Savina Princen https://www.cairn.info/revue-reflets-et-perspectives-de-la-vie-economique-2012-3-page-161.htm

Reclaiming corporate tax revenues https://www.epi.org/publication/reclai ming-corporate-tax-revenues/

Tax Planning For Beginners: 6 Key Principles Explained https://www.botk eeper.com/blog/tax-planning-for-beginners-6-key-principles-explained

The Principles of Proactive Tax Planning [Five Considerations for Business Owners] https://warrenaverett.com/insights/the-principles-of-proactive-tax-planning-five-considerations-for-business-owners/

Four Reasons to Align Your Supply Chain and Tax Strategies https://www.b do.com/insights/tax/four-reasons-to-align-your-supply-chain-and-tax-strategies

How do you balance risk and reward in decision making? https://www.link edin.com/advice/0/how-do-you-balance-risk-reward-decision-making

Balancing risk and reward: How C-suite leaders can innovate responsibly https://www.fastcompany.com/90977835/balancing-risk-and-reward-ho w-c-suite-leaders-can-innovate-responsibly

Tax Planning Process https://www.stptax.com/tax-planning/tax-plannin g-process/

What is tax planning? https://www.dsaprospect.co.uk/guides/tax-plannin g

Tax planning process https://taxfitness.com.au/tax-planning/tax-planni ng-process/

4-step process for tax planning https://www.farmprogress.com/manage ment/4-step-process-for-tax-planning

Tax Credit vs. Deduction: What's the Difference? Both reduce your tax bill—but in different ways https://www.wsj.com/buyside/personal-finance/ tax-credit-vs-deduction-6f611898

Tax Deductions & Credits https://www.investopedia.com/tax-deductions-

and-credits-4689689

What Is Tax Avoidance and How Is It Different From Tax Evasion? https://w
ww.investopedia.com/terms/t/tax_avoidance.asp

Minimize taxes and maximize your bottom line https://www.investopedia.
com/articles/stocks/11/intro-tax-efficient-investing.asp

Tax-Exempt Interest Definition and Examples https://www.investopedia.c
om/terms/t/taxexemptinterest.asp

Retirement Contribution: Meaning, Types, Limits https://www.investoped
ia.com/terms/r/retirement-contribution.asp

Tax Break Definition, Different Types, How to Get One https://www.invest
opedia.com/terms/t/tax-break.asp

How to get the most money back on your tax return https://www.invest
opedia.com/financial-edge/0312/how-to-get-the-most-money-back-on-
your-tax-return.aspx

Tax Credit: What It Is, How It Works, What Qualifies, 3 Types https://www.
investopedia.com/terms/t/taxcredit.asp

23 Income Tax Incentives for Investment https://www.imf.org/external/
pubs/nft/1998/tlaw/eng/ch23.pdf

Understanding Business Expenses and Which Are Tax Deductible https://w
ww.investopedia.com/terms/b/businessexpenses.asp

Deductible vs. Non-deductible Business Expenses https://www.sorgecpa.c
om/resources/insights/deductible-vs.-non-deductible-business-expenses

Ordinary and Necessary Expense: What it is, How it Works https://www.inv
estopedia.com/terms/o/oandne.asp

Amortization vs. Depreciation: What's the Difference? https://www.inves
topedia.com/ask/answers/06/amortizationvsdepreciation.asp#:~:text=Am
ortization%20and%20depreciation%20are%20two,to%20reflect%20its%
20anticipated%20deterioration

Amortization vs. Depreciation: What's the Difference? https://www.inves
topedia.com/ask/answers/06/amortizationvsdepreciation.asp#:~:text=Am
ortization%20and%20depreciation%20are%20two,to%20reflect%20its%
20anticipated%20deterioration

R&D Tax Credits and Deductions https://pro.bloombergtax.com/brief/rdtax-credit-and-deducting-rd-expenditures/

Renewable Energy Credits (RECs), Explained https://watchwire.ai/renewa ble-energy-credits-recs-explained/#:~:text=So%2C%20What%20Exactly %20Are%20Renewable,power%20lines%20that%20transport%20energy.

Navigating the World of Taxation: A Comprehensive Guide https://www.lin kedin.com/pulse/navigating-world-taxation-comprehensive-guide#:~:tex t=Intriguingly%2C%20the%20considerations%20of%20residency,shape% 20the%20international%20tax%20landscape

Transfer Pricing: What It Is and How It Works, With Examples https://ww w.investopedia.com/terms/t/transfer-pricing.asp

International Tax Planning and Compliance https://www.hco.com/insight s/international-tax-planning-and-compliance

Guidance Note Compliance Risk Management: Managing and Improving Tax Compliance https://www.oecd.org/tax/administration/33818656.pdf

How Tax Treaties Prevent Tax Leakage in Cross-Border Projects https://w ww.huntonak.com/en/insights/how-tax-treaties-prevent-tax-leakage-in-cross-border-projects.html

Improving Tax Compliance: Establishing a Risk Management Framework https://www.adb.org/publications/improving-tax-compliance

Internal Audit and Tax Compliance https://myusf.usfca.edu/internal-audit

Internal Control System and Tax Compliance: An Empirical Analysis https://www.ijicc.net/images/vol11iss12/111204_Prawira_2020_E_R.pdf

Navigating Tax Risks in Indirect Tax: A Strategic Guide for Risk Management https://www.complyiq.io/navigating-tax-risks/

The promise and limitations of information technology for tax mobilization https://blogs.worldbank.org/developmenttalk/promise-and-limitations-i nformation-technology-tax-mobilization

Information Technology for Tax Administration https://pdf.usaid.gov/pdf_ docs/pnaea485.pdf

5 Tax Planning Examples https://www.modwm.com/5-tax-planning-exa mples/

4 global tax trends and how they impact your operations https://www.tm f-group.com/en/news-insights/articles/2019/april/global-tax-trend-and-

impact-your-operations/

About the Author

Professor Uwem Essia is a distinguished academic and celebrated author known for his illustrious career in leadership, management, economics, and development. Since June 2021, Professor Essia has immersed himself in personal studies and established himself as a prolific online book publisher, with a presence on platforms. He holds a PhD degree in Economics. Professor Uwem Essia's career is a testament to his passion for knowledge, education, and the betterment of society. His vast experience, research contributions, and dedication to fostering positive change make him a prominent figure in leadership, management, and economics. With a wealth of knowledge and a commitment to academic excellence, Professor Essia continues to make a significant impact. He is open to collaboration in joint research work/consulting, Adjunct and remote teaching, theses/dissertation supervision, professorial assessment, article/book editing and previewing, and joint book and article publishing.

You can connect with me on:

🌐 https://digitalgainspro.com

📘 https://www.facebook.com/uwem.essia.3

🔗 https://www.amazon.com/author/uwemessia

Also by Uwem Essia

History of Economic Thought

"History of Economic Thought" is a captivating journey through the evolution of economic thoughts that have profoundly shaped our world. Notably, this book has extended the history of economic thought to the paradigm shifts and new thinking occasioned by the COVID-19 pandemic that has made revolutionary alterations in the behavior of individuals, firms/organizations, and states compelling. The book is organized into five parts and twenty-nine chapters, exploring economic ideas, theories, and debates from the ancient moral and religious discourses to the modern paradigms and policy imperatives in a rapidly changing global landscape. The book delves into the influential contributions of key figures as they challenged, revolutionized, and reshaped economic ideologies. Explore the transition from classical economics to neoclassical foundations and witness the paradigm shifts prompted by unprecedented events like the Great Depression, the 2008 financial crisis, and the COVID-19 pandemic. This book is a comprehensive exploration of the past, present, and future of economic theory and policy, offering profound insights into the forces that have driven economic progress and transformation throughout history up to the current period.

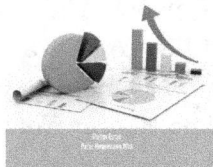

Economic Development Planning

"Economic Development Planning: Theory and Practice" is an in-depth exploration of the theories, strategies, and components essential for effective economic development. The book is organized into twelve sections with forty-nine chapters, covering various topics that collectively provide a comprehensive understanding of planned economic growth and development. From an overview of economic development theories, it then delves into practical aspects of economic development planning, discussing resource utilization, infrastructure development, human capital investment, and sustainable development. The book also emphasizes the importance of balanced development, regional growth, and inclusive decision-making and promotes modeling approaches like the Theory of Change, Logical Framework, and Result-Based Management. It addresses crucial aspects such as project financing, innovative funding approaches, and private-sector engagement. In sum, this book is a comprehensive package aiming to equip its readers with the knowledge and tools necessary to navigate the multifaceted challenges and opportunities of economic development in today's globalized world.

Principles of Corporate Finance

Principles of Corporate Finance, a comprehensive exploration and an enlightening guide, meticulously crafted for students and finance professionals, unveils the intricate layers of corporate finance theory, strategic applications, and ethical considerations. Each chapter equips readers with indispensable knowledge, from tracing the historical evolution of finance to navigating modern challenges like ESG integration, risk management, and financial crises. The book has thirty-eight chapters organized into ten parts that explore the various dimensions of corporate finance theory, practice, and impact. It delves into financial statement analysis, time value of money principles, and crucial decision-making strategies. Uncover the complexities of mergers, acquisitions, and value creation while mastering stock and bond valuation. Beyond theory, this book addresses the ethical dimensions of corporate governance, business ethics, and social responsibility. Whether as a student seeking insights or a finance professional navigating the evolving landscape, 'Principles of Corporate Finance' is our essential guide to understanding and using corporate finance concepts and tools in your studies/research and professional practice.